M

WITH

DATE DUE

The Two of Us

. . . AND FRIENDS

The Two of Us

. . . AND FRIENDS

A Young Couple's Guide
to Cooking and Entertaining
(Easily, Affordably) with Elegance and Style

Written and Illustrated by

JESSIE CARRY SAUNDERS

MARLOWE & COMPANY
NEW YORK

THE TWO OF US . . . AND FRIENDS:
A Young Couple's Guide to Cooking and Entertaining
(Easily, Affordably) with Elegance and Style

Text and Illustrations copyright © 2006 by Jessie Carry Saunders

Published by
Marlowe & Company
An Imprint of Avalon Publishing Group, Incorporated
245 West 17th Street • 11th floor
New York, NY 10011

Library of Congress Cataloging-in-Publication Data

Saunders, Jessie Carry, 1976-
    The two of us . . . and friends : a young couple's guide to cooking and entertaining
(easily, affordably) with elegance and style / Jessie Carry Saunders.
        p. cm.
    ISBN 1-56924-325-5 (hardcover)
    1. Entertaining.   2. Cookery.   I. Title.
    TX731.S323 2006
    641.5—dc22

                                                                        2006018146

                    ISBN-10: 1-56924-325-5
                    ISBN-13: 978-1-56924-325-1

                    9 8 7 6 5 4 3 2 1

Designed by Pauline Neuwirth, Neuwirth & Associates, Inc.

Printed in China

To Mom and Pops

Thanks for buying me that Easy-Bake Oven

Contents

The Joy of Six

Eight and Up

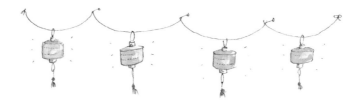

Acknowledgments

Thank you to Mom and Pop, Will, Aunt Debbie, and Patty, for endless cooking and entertaining consultations. Thank you to all the guinea pigs, including Jordan and Pierre, Dune and Mike, Isabelle and Ronnie, Callie and Thomas, Joyce, Weatherly, Jamie and Kristina, Josh, and David. Thank you to everyone past and present who worked on this book at Marlowe & Company, particularly my publisher, Matthew Lore, my editor Katie McHugh, Kylie Foxx, and Wendie Carr for all her work with publicity. Thanks to Susi Olberhelman for the cover, and Pauline Neuwirth of Neuwirth and Associates for the seamless book design. Thank you also to Rich Berman at Richard Berman PR for all his hard work. The most thanks go to my agent, Janis Donnaud, for her wisdom and support; and to Johnny, whose unflagging enthusiasm for eating my food makes me the luckiest cook alive.

The Two of Us

. . . AND FRIENDS

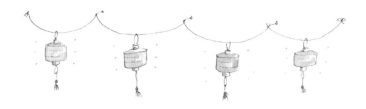

Introduction

Getting a seat around our kitchen table is hard. Literally. In our tiny apartment, with its Greenwich Village idiosyncrasies (the bathroom opens into the kitchen, the floors slope alarmingly, the walls seem to be made of old newspaper, et cetera), it's physically difficult to squeeze many chairs around our three-foot-square kitchen table.

The general rule is to fit six people, maximum, but we've gotten as many as nine shoehorned in there. This feat involved my husband, JS, dismantling my desk for extra table space, and using our bedside tables (themselves repurposed Chinese garden seats from a junk store in Queens) as extra seating. If anybody needed to get up, for any reason, the entire table had to stand up, too. Everyone had a great time.

You may be asking yourself, what is the point of this little story?

I guess it's that nothing stops me from giving a party, and that nothing—lack of experience, lack of crockery, lack of seating—should keep you from throwing one, either. Nothing is more human and more fun than entertaining yourselves at home, and few things are more appreciated by your guests than a bit of extra effort put out on their behalf.

Now you might be asking yourself, Who is this girl and why should I listen to her?

Well, because I'm just like you, except I've spent too much time in front of the stove. I don't have any degrees from world-famous cooking institutions, but I've fed a lot of people a lot of food at home, and I've picked up a useful trick or two for getting through a dinner party with ease and a bit of style.

I learned from a master, my father (who played a prominent role in my first cookbook, *Not on Love Alone*), a man who can cook, pour the wine, and tell a great story simultaneously. For many years, I was his sous-chef, the person in charge of resting the sprig of parsley on a plate or wiping the rim of a dish when a spot of sauce was misladled. From him, I learned the basics of being a good hostess. So when, right out of college, I threw a few dinner parties, it was good to be the queen. I knew what to do and I was proud to do it.

But my real dinner party days didn't emerge until JS and I were living together in the aforementioned Greenwich Village railroad apartment and trying out our his-and-her social patter for the first time. There JS was, pouring glasses of wine! There I was, actually remembering to wear an apron over my new skirt! There we were, arguing about what music to put on (my stance? No Led Zeppelin before eleven o'clock).

It soon became clear that entertaining together was different from when I had been the captain of the ship. There was more give-and-take, and perhaps I had to make a few compromises (not always my strong suit), but at the same time it was easier—there were two of us, remembering things the other forgot (like the bottle of wine about to explode in the freezer) and sharing cleanup duties after everyone was gone. Entertaining as a team makes you a better party-thrower, since the responsibility for everyone's good time isn't wholly yours.

There are only a few golden rules in entertaining at home. First, don't panic, no matter what happens—with the possible exception of the arrival of the Fire Department. Kitchen disasters can be fixed or pizza can be ordered. Second, don't try to do everything yourself. For small parties, it can be the two of you manning the stove, or groups of friends pooling their resources (both of money and time) and getting together to celebrate occasions big and small in backyards and living rooms. Finally, don't quit. If your first party isn't a rip-roaring success, give yourself (and your significant other) a break. Try and try again—you'll get the hang of it.

Which brings me to the nuts-and-bolts of this cookbook. The four sections that follow this introduction—The Two of You, Party of Four, Joy of Six, and For Eight and Up—let you dip a toe into throwing dinners, first by getting used to cooking for just two, and then, slowly but surely, adding friends and family until everybody you know is over at your house and asking where the corkscrew is. Along the way, there are sidebars and boxes filled with information on entertaining calmly and wisely, and some crafty projects—all Styrofoam ball and glue gun-free—to decorate your table and party spaces. I've also tried to guide you, step-by-step, through the more elaborate parties.

This book is filled with thoughts I've had and solutions I've developed for entertaining easily and with personality. But it's my personality, and it can be quirky. For instance: I like to eat my salad after the main course. It's how we did it growing up, and there's a great rhythm to a meal when it can meander toward dessert. When you host a dinner party, you and your mate are running around for the first half, filling glasses and making sure the roast isn't overcooked. But after the main course, you can really relax and get into great conversations. Serving the salad at that stage of the meal is a perfect conversation-enabler. Here's something else I like to do: put on some dance tunes during dessert. A little chocolate cake, a little Mariah Carey—what could be better? And it's a nice transition away from the table. This is my dinner-party style, and I'm happy to share it with you. But I encourage you to find your own happy entertaining style, so that you, too, will always want to squeeze one more chair around your kitchen table.

Top Five Basics You Need in Your Kitchen, Utensils Version

1. A large skillet
2. A generously sized saucepan
3. A 6-inch chef's knife
4. A colander
5. A set of tongs

Top Five Basics You Need in Your Kitchen, Larder Version*

1. Canned plum tomatoes
2. Kosher salt
3. A dozen eggs
4. Olive oil
5. Dijon mustard

*And you should always have all-purpose flour and baking soda, even if you never use them.

Party Pantry

This is a list of ten items that I've found extraordinarily helpful as a hostess. I always have them on hand. They range from the obvious to the less so.

UNSCENTED VOTIVE CANDLES: Overhead light on full blast? Scary and unflattering. Nonsmelly candles flickering attractively over the faces of your friends while they eat? A thing of beauty.

PISTACHIO NUTS AND OLIVES: Instant apéritif snacks, for when company is unexpected or you just plain forgot to get something.

COFFEE AND TEA: For people after dinner. Though I'm terrible at making coffee (more on that later) it's polite to offer, and tea really can help you digest your dinner.

CHAMPAGNE: Because it's nice to be frivolous and have a bottle waiting in the fridge, just in case there's something wonderful to celebrate.

CLUB SODA: To drink, if you want, but I use it along with table salt as a quick fix in any wine/tablecloth emergency.

DIET COKE AND CRANBERRY JUICE: My choices, along with bubbly water, for nondrinker drinks. It's important to have something on hand other than lukewarm tap water for those who prefer not to imbibe.

AUNT PEGGY'S SPAGHETTI: This is a recipe on page 119. I mention it here because the sauce keeps forever in the freezer and, if you always have a spare box of spaghetti around, you can feed surprise guests or surprise vegetarians.

WATER GLASSES: Even if someone's drinking wine, remember to give them a glass for water, too. I know it sounds silly but it happens all the time that I have wine and no water, and the results aren't pretty. So give your guests the option! They might be thirsty.

EXTRA NAPKINS: Because someone might lose one or soak one in Diet Coke—you can't ask them to use their pants leg for a napkin the rest of the night.

CHOCOLATES: When making dessert is beyond you, a few chocolates passed around the table never fail to please.

A Week in the Life

*D*ays *of the* week, and what they're good for, party-wise.

SUNDAY:

A perfect lazy brunch or lunch day, particularly in the fall when there's football on and you need some friends to hold your hand as the New York Jets lose again.

MONDAY:

Since there's no greater relief then getting through a Monday, this is the perfect night to eat together and relax alone.

TUESDAY:

Tuesday night is the real nadir of the week, socially. You should probably just chuck it all and go eat popcorn at the movies.

WEDNESDAY:

An excellent night for an impromptu dinner with one or two friends. Nothing fancy has to happen here—just a dish of pasta and a glass of red wine.

THURSDAY:

Always seems a night for going out—anticipating a lazy Friday, perhaps—so a prime candidate for the late-night meal.

FRIDAY:

Having six or more people over for dinner is mostly an end-of-week exercise. If you plan well, you can get a bunch of cooking done ahead of time on Thursday, and have Friday evening to set the table, do some cosmetic vacuuming, and pour pistachio nuts into bowls.

SATURDAY:

The easiest day to throw a blow-out party, depending on your work schedule. You'll need all day to shop, organize, and cook, and some friends to help you.

The Two of You

A Simple Supper

Sweet-and-Sour Tomato Salad (page 11)
Spaghetti Carbonara à la Grandma (page 12) or
Carbonara-Primavera (page 14) or
Baked Carbonara (page 16)
Wilted Spinach Salad with Garlic Dressing (page 19)
Earl Grey Granita (page 21)
Sugar and Spice Cookies (page 22)

You like to cook—on Saturday night. You enjoy time in front of the stove—on Sunday afternoon. But Wednesday? Are you kidding?

Well, get ready, because I'm here to spread the word: weekday cooking is not only possible, it's fun. Nobody expects beef Wellington mid-week. But an elegant, low-maintenance meal—a nice plate of pasta, a glass of red wine, and maybe a touch of dessert—whether you make it for two, or add a sibling or last-minute friend, is a little gift in the middle of otherwise routine nights.

The easiest way to do this is to start with an ingredient that practically makes itself: spaghetti. The simple sauces—those with little or no cooking involved—can be made while the pasta boils, and then it's just an issue of a quickly set table, a bit of nice lighting, and you've got yourself a civilized meal.

Sweet-and-Sour Tomato Salad

$\mathcal{T}$HIS SALAD MAKES use of a great modern achievement: the sweet, tangy cherry tomato, perfect for eating year round. Unlike regular tomatoes, which out of season tend to be mealy, these babies are always firm and juicy, and usually on prominent display in your local super-market. The sweet-and-sour dressing is a nice change from the traditional olive-oil-and-basil tomato treatment.

- 1 pint cherry or grape tomatoes
- 1 small clove garlic
- 2 teaspoons salad oil (I like canola or grapeseed)

2 teaspoons red wine vinegar
1 teaspoon sugar
Salt and pepper

1. Rinse and drain the tomatoes, then slice them in half, or, if they're particularly large, into quarters. They should be bite-size. Set aside.
2. Grate the garlic into a bowl that will be large enough to hold the tomatoes, and then add the oil, red wine vinegar, sugar, and salt and pepper to taste. The dressing should be quite tart, since there's ample sweetness in the tomatoes themselves.
3. Add the tomatoes and toss to coat. You can eat this right away, but it's perfectly fine to let it sit for the time it takes you to make pasta—the flavors deepen and mingle.

TIME: *About 5 minutes, and an option for 10 more if you'd like the tomatoes to marinate*
FEEDS: *2, as a side dish or first course*

Pasta #1

Spaghetti Carbonara à la Grandma

*I*TALIAN FOOD HAS always been about Grandma, and it always will be. This old-world carbonara is as old-fashioned as you get, and quick. You'll be thrilled with the results: a spaghetti dish lightly coated but strongly flavored with egg yolk, bacon, and cheese. The ingredients are not too expensive, so consider stocking up on some artisanal pastas—brands like De Cecco or Latini, found at your more upscale gourmet food stores—if you're feeling fancy.

- ¼ pound slab bacon or pancetta, cut into matchstick-size pieces
- ½ pound (about ½ package) spaghetti
- 3 egg yolks (freeze the whites for another recipe; for instance, Chocolate Floating Island, page 112)
- ¼ cup heavy cream or crème fraîche, or even plain yogurt

- ½ cup freshly grated Parmesan cheese (plus extra for serving)
- ¼ cup freshly grated Romano cheese
- Salt and pepper
- A handful of chopped fresh parsley

1. Bring a large pot of water to a boil for the pasta. While the water's heating, render the bacon in a small skillet over low heat. The low heat will allow for the most fat to melt out and will prevent the bacon from burning. Remove the pieces of meat with a slotted spoon and let them drain on a paper towel or clean brown paper bag.

2. When the water is boiling, throw in a palmful of kosher salt and then the spaghetti. Cook according to package directions, but start checking the pasta a minute or two minutes before they advise—al dente is the name of the game in carbonara.

3. Meanwhile, in a large bowl, mix the egg yolks and cream until combined. Add the cheeses, a few grindings of pepper, and a pinch of salt (be careful not to add too much, because the cheese and the bacon are both salty). If you're wondering about raw egg yolks, don't worry-the warmth of the pasta will heat the yolks past the point of fear.

4. Finally, when the pasta's done (but not too done!) drain the pasta and throw it in the bowl. Immediately start tossing with the egg yolk mixture, so that the yolks turn into a satiny sauce instead of scrambling. Keep tossing.

5. After you're satisfied that all the strands are equally coated, add the pancetta bits and the parsley, taste the spaghetti, adjust the salt if necessary, and toss again. Serve piping hot, in shallow bowls for ease of eating.

TIME: *As much as it takes your stove to heat the spaghetti water, plus about 10 minutes*
FEEDS: *2, plus lunch for 1 the next day*

YOLKING IT UP:
HOW TO SEPARATE AN EGG

*T*HE POLITE WAY to separate an egg is to use the cracked shell as two cups, sliding the yolk back and forth between the two until all the white has separated. Unfortunately, when I do this, I always manage to break the yolks—not dire in Spaghetti Carbonara's circumstance, but if you need the white and not the yolk, well, it causes a lot of swearing, because your egg whites need to be impeccably pure. So separate as I do, caveman style. Forget the dainty shells, and slide the egg into your cupped palms, allowing the egg whites to slip through without puncturing a yolk. Of course, if you fancy yourself Betty Crocker, your average housewares store sells an egg separator that can take the place of your fingers.

Pasta #2

Carbonara-Primavera

$\mathcal{P}$LEASE BE HONEST. Do you (or your significant other) eat enough vegetables? Are you a model of FDA food-pyramid faithfulness? No . . . I thought not. Nor am I, and I love vegetables. And I try to behave. I do. But sometimes you can't eat another salad, and have to come up with ingenious ways to eat more healthily. My non-FDA approved (but Homer Simpson approved) way? Mix vegetables with bacon.

1 tablespoon unsalted butter

3 medium-size carrots, peeled and cut on the diagonal into ¼-inch-thick ovals

1 medium-size zucchini, washed, not peeled, halved lengthwise, and sliced into ⅓-inch-thick half-moons

⅔ cup frozen baby peas

¼ pound slab bacon or pancetta, cut into matchstick-size pieces

½ pound fusilli or farfalle

3 egg yolks

¼ cup heavy cream or crème fraîche

½ cup freshly grated Parmesan cheese

½ cup chopped fresh herbs, including parsley and basil (you can also include a bit of marjoram, if you can find it, or oregano)

Salt and pepper

1. Start by bringing a large pot of water to a boil. Then, in a shallow saucepan or a skillet with a lid, combine the butter and carrots with ½ cup of water and a pinch of salt, and cover, cooking over lively heat for 5 to 7 minutes, until the steam comes hissing out the sides of the lid and the carrots are beginning to turn tender. Remove the lid, add the zukes, and cook for another 5 minutes. You want all the liquid to boil away, leaving just a bit of a buttery glaze on the vegetables. Add the peas and stir for about a minute, then turn off the heat.

2. Prepare the bacon by sautéing in a small skillet over low heat, until all the fat is rendered away. Remove with a slotted spoon and drain on a paper towel or a clean brown paper bag. (For those who want to reduce the number of dirty pans, just render the bacon in the pan you plan on using for the veggies, and wipe the pan clean with paper towels before adding the carrots.)

3. When the pasta water is boiling, add a palmful of kosher salt and throw in the fusilli. Then, in a large bowl, combine the egg yolks with the cream, the Parmesan, a healthy dose of freshly ground pepper, and a good pinch of salt. Right before the pasta is ready, add the vegetables and stir to coat. Then throw in the pasta and give it a good turn in the sauce right away (tongs come in very handy here).
4. Taste and correct for salt, then add the bacon and the chopped herbs, toss again, and serve hot to your veggie-loving, bacon-eating selves.

TIME: *About 30 minutes, some unattended*
FEEDS: *2, with extra to throw in a frittata the next day (try the Side-Dish Frittata on page 58)*

MULTIPLICATION TABLE:
Spaghetti

HERE'S A PERSON who made a fortune selling plastic squares with variously sized circles punched in them-spaghetti measuring templates, so you have just enough for two, four, six, and so on. I kid not. Note to self: become an inventor.

Anyway, if you have a hankering to make these recipes for a larger group—and pasta is always a crowd pleaser—you can double them, minus one egg yolk, or triple them, minus two egg yolks.

Pasta #3
Baked Carbonara

THIS IS ACTUALLY JS's, favorite of the three, and I can't blame him. Of course, since you have to turn on the oven, it's more of a fall/winter dish than a spring/summer dish, but there are chilly nights when nothing's better than an old-fashioned baked pasta dish. Prepare yourself for a second helping.

1 tablespoon olive oil

⅓ cup slab bacon or pancetta, cut into matchstick-size pieces

8 ounces fresh white mushrooms, cleaned and quartered

½ pound ziti or penne

1½ cups whole or 2% milk

3 tablespoons unsalted butter

2 tablespoons all-purpose flour

3 egg yolks, lightly beaten

1½ teaspoons kosher salt

Pepper

½ cup chopped fresh parsley

⅓ cup ricotta cheese

½ cup freshly grated Parmesan cheese

½ cup dried bread crumbs

1. Preheat the oven to 375°F. Bring a large pot of water to a boil. While it's coming up to temperature, heat a skillet over medium-high heat, pour in the oil, then throw in the pancetta, shuffling the pan a bit to loosen any pieces that might stick. When the pancetta starts to brown—things should be very lively in the pan—throw in the quartered mushrooms, and toss to coat in the fat. Let the mushrooms brown for about 3 minutes, then add a pinch of salt, stir, and remove from the heat.

2. Throw the pasta into the boiling water and cook it 2 or 3 minutes less than the directions on the package.

3. Heat the milk. I like to do this in the microwave to avoid using another pan, but be careful! It's much more painful to clean boiled-over milk out of your microwave than to wash an extra pan. In any case, you need the milk to be hot but not boiling; everyone's microwave is different, so use your own experience in this case.

4. For the sauce: melt 2 tablespoons of the butter over medium heat in a medium-size saucepan. When the foam subsides, add the flour, and stir continuously for

a minute until the roux (as this butter and flour combo is called) is nonlumpy and the flour has cooked. Here's the only tricky bit: in a slow but steady stream, pour the hot milk into the roux, stirring all the while, and fighting the good fight against any lumps threatening to form. When the milk is completely incorporated, cook the sauce—this is basic béchamel—over medium-high heat, stirring, making sure to work the entire surface area of the pot, until it thickens, about 5 minutes. It should have the consistency of heavy cream.

5. Take a spoonful or two of the béchamel out of the pot and mix it with the egg yolks, to temper them—this means they won't scramble. Then pour the egg yolks back into the béchamel, and stir until the sauce is uniform. Add the salt and some pepper, then the mushrooms mixture and parsley, and, when it's ready, the pasta.

6. Spread half of the pasta into an 8-inch square baking dish (or something similarly sized). Dot the top with the ricotta, and sprinkle with half the Parmesan cheese. Add the rest of the pasta, then top with the bread crumbs, the rest of the Parm, and dots of the remaining tablespoon of butter. Throw that puppy into the oven and bake for 25 minutes, until it's golden brown and bubbly.

TIME: *About 40 minutes*
FEEDS: *2, heartily*

BAKED PASTA ADD-INS

*O*HH, BAKED PASTA dishes. So warm, so good, so creamy, so crunchy. Old fashioned or not, my love will never die. Using the Baked Carbonara recipe above as a guide, you can augment your lovely dinner in the following ways:

SMOKED HAM   or   SHREDDED CHICKEN   or   RED ONION

Today's Dinner, Tomorrow's Lunch

My friend Jordan has a neurosis: she can't eat leftovers or, as she calls it, "old food." She is at a loss to explain why—the universal scrunched-nose-and-curled-lip facial expression is explanation enough, I guess. But I'm an avid supporter of eating leftovers, as long as they're attractively repurposed. I understand that the microwaved gelatinous mass formerly known as last night's beef stew can be very unappealing, but if you spent any time, effort, and money making that stew in the first place, it's worth eating before it becomes an inhabitant in another mystery food sarcophagus in the back of your fridge. So make that beef stew into a nice ragout for egg noodles-and that leftover carbonara the filling of a tasty frittata. Very quick, and tasty enough to fool Jordan.

MONDAY:

POT ROAST

TUESDAY:

PASTA SAUCE

ZITI CARBONARA

ZITI FRITTATA

Wilted Spinach Salad with Garlic Dressing

*T*HIS IS A salad that you can dress while the pasta is cooking, and it only gets better and tastier as it sits, as opposed to every other salad in the world that only gets slimier and droopier after dressing.

1 tablespoon extra-virgin olive oil

1 clove garlic, thoroughly crushed

2 teaspoons Dijon mustard

½ lemon

3 cups fresh spinach, washed, stemmed, and dried (the bagged sort comes in very handy in these situations)

Sea salt and pepper

1. In a large skillet, heat the olive oil and crushed garlic over medium heat, until you can really smell the garlic but it hasn't turned brown, about a minute.
2. Remove the garlic clove, and swirl the Dijon mustard into the oil. Turn off the heat and squeeze the juice of your half-lemon into the dressing. Add about 1 teaspoon of sea salt and plenty of freshly ground pepper. Give it a stir.
3. Put the prepped spinach in a salad bowl, and pour the warm dressing over the top, giving the whole lot a good spin. Taste for salt, then take it to the table.

TIME: *About 10 minutes, including washing the spinach*
FEEDS: *2*

The Basics
Weekday Eating

Though there's a full menu here, there are times when life and work intervene and and you don't have enough time for the whole shebang. If you can't manage every last detail, try making one course, which easily becomes two courses if you throw in a little cheese or dessert at the end. Add in thirty seconds of table setting and thirty minutes or so of lazy cooking while you talk to your cousin on the telephone, we're not talking huge imposition of time. That said, you should try to sit down for more than ten minutes: scarfing isn't the point.

And I'm not forcing Vivaldi and candlelight down your throat, either. I'll admit that sometimes, during baseball season, if the Mets haven't yet broken my heart, the game will be on in the background. JS is very patient with me. But at least we're sitting and eating together, which makes the bit of effort very worthwhile.

Earl Grey Granita

THIS SHERBETLIKE CONCOCTION is really delicious freshly made—the vanilla and the bergamot in the Earl Grey are a potent combination. Try to eat as much as you can the day you make it, however, because after a day or two it becomes less granita, and more ice.

3 tea bags Earl Grey tea   Scant 1/2 cup sugar
1/4 vanilla bean, sliced in half lengthwise

1. Boil 2 cups of water in a saucepan, then remove from the heat. Dangle the tea bags in the water and let them steep for 5 minutes.
2. Remove the tea bags, and add the vanilla bean and the sugar, stirring constantly with a wooden spoon until the sugar is completely dissolved. Pour the mixture into a shallow casserole or metal baking pan (you want one wide and shallow, not small and deep). Let the tea mixture cool on your counter for 30 minutes.
3. Slide the lukewarm tea into the freezer; then, for the next 2 hours, give the tea a careful stir every 20 minutes. At the end of the 2 hours, you can leave the granita alone to finish setting for another hour. To serve, scrape up the granita with the side of a spoon, mounding the crystals into a little bowl.

TIME: *About 3 hours, mostly unattended*
FEEDS: *2*

Sugar and Spice Cookies

CRUMBLY AND SWEET, these cookies add a kick to the Earl Grey Granita, on nights when the granita doesn't sate your sweet tooth. These cookies are also perfect with ice cream or coffee, and the recipe makes plenty to share with friends.

2 cups unbleached all-purpose flour

1 1/4 teaspoons baking powder

2 teaspoons ground ginger

1/2 teaspoon freshly ground nutmeg

1/2 teaspoon ground allspice

1/2 teaspoon ground cardamom

1/4 teaspoon ground cloves

Pinch of salt

6 tablespoons (3/4 stick) unsalted butter, softened

3/4 cup brown sugar

1 egg, plus 1 egg white for glazing

1 teaspoon vanilla extract

1 teaspoon Grand Marnier or other orange-flavored liqueur (optional)

Zest of 1/2 orange

1/3 cup granulated sugar

1. Lay out a large piece of waxed paper on your countertop, grab your flour sifter or a fine-mesh sieve, and sift together the flour, baking powder, ginger, nutmeg, allspice, cardamom, cloves, and salt.
2. Cream the butter and the brown sugar in the bowl of your food processor or by hand with a wooden spoon, then add the egg, vanilla extract, Grand Marnier, and orange zest. Zip the mixture around until it is combined. Add the flour mixture in several batches until the dough is smooth and uniform.
3. Turn the dough—it will be a bit crumbly—back onto that piece of waxed paper you used to sift the flour. Mold it into a log, and put it in the refrigerator—or better yet, the freezer—for at least 1 hour. Take the dough out of the fridge and lightly flour the cutting board. Divide the dough into fourths, then roll each fourth into to a log about 2 inches in diameter. Put the logs back in the fridge. (You can freeze the dough at this stage—wrap it in aluminum foil first—and use when you want straight from the freezer, but within a month).
4. Preheat the oven to 350°F. Lightly grease two cookie sheets.

5. Mix the egg white with a teaspoon of water, just to break it up a bit. Put the granulated sugar on a dinner plate.

6. Fetch the dough logs and carefully roll them, one by one, in the egg white, then in the sugar. Place on a cutting board and, using a sharp knife, cut the logs into slices about ⅓ inch thick.

7. Lay the cookies about 2 inches apart on a prepared sheet and bake for 11 to 13 minutes, or until they turn golden at the edges. Remove from the oven and immediately transfer the cookies to a wire rack to cool completely. They'll keep in an airtight container for a week or more.

TIME: *A few hours to allow the dough to set up, but about 20 minutes actual baking time*

FEEDS: *Makes 4 dozen 2-inch cookies (see note)*

SPECIAL EQUIPMENT: *A food processor makes these cookies come together in minutes.*

NOTE: *Feel like a few cookies, not forty-eight? Bake a fourth of the dough at a time, about one cookie sheet's worth, and keep the rest in the freezer for whenever you want it. Baking the dough straight from the freezer will add a minute or two to the baking time.*

Thirty Seconds to Set a Table

*H*ere are *nine* items that you should plunk on your kitchen table when you're sitting down to eat on a weekday, so you don't have to get up nine times during dinner to fetch them:

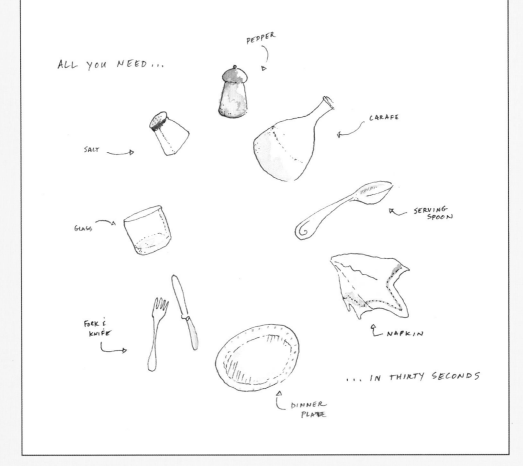

ALL YOU NEED...

PEPPER

SALT

CARAFE

GLASS

SERVING SPOON

FORK & KNIFE

NAPKIN

DINNER PLATE

... IN THIRTY SECONDS

Flower Power
ROSEMARY

UNLESS YOU'RE ELTON John and have a $100,000-a-month flower budget, weekdays are not a time that you'll splurge on elaborate floral arrangements or flowers that are five bucks a stem. However, that bunch of rosemary you bought for $1.99 makes an admirable centerpiece if you use a bit of panache. Just select the most beautiful and interesting-looking branches, trim the bottoms if they're very long, and arrange them in a pretty vase or cup, preferably one that's not clear glass. Not only does your table become prettier, it smells prettier, too.

FROM THE SUPERMARKET.

STRIP THE STEMS

... TO THE BUD VASE

Birthday Dinner à Deux

Shallot Tarte Tatin (page 27)
Pork Chops Milanese (page 29)
Apple and Celery Root Salad (page 31)
Cheese and Walnuts
Carrot Cakelettes with Lemon Icing (page 32)

I know that some people get very grumpy about birthdays, but I don't see why. No matter how old you are, there are two birthday constants that make the day better than any other day: presents and birthday cake. I love presents (just for the record, in case you were thinking of sending me something on August 24, I prefer wrapped presents. Items shoved into gift bags take away half the fun of guessing what's inside). And I love cake, particularly slightly lopsided, iced-with-love homemade cakes. I know there are people out there who agree with me, and who frankly push the whole birthday thing to the limit. A friend of mine insists on a full week of celebration, but if she can hornswoggle her friends and loved ones into going along with it, I say "brava."

With this menu, I make an argument for the third birthday constant—an intimate dinner for two, with just enough extra effort to make it something out the ordinary. The little touches—the pretty salad with the chops, the time spent arranging the caramelized shallots—will speak volumes about your love and devotion. The crowning glory of this menu is the cake. Every year for JS's birthday I am called upon to commune with Betty Crocker. His love for the chemically yellow cake-mix cake, complete with rubbery canned icing, is deeply ingrained, and seems impervious to my attempts to woo him with examples with slightly fewer preservative agents. But my choice is carrot cake, with a lot of yummy goodies inside. And for those who miss the sunny yellow cake mix, this cake is naturally orange, without a drop artificial food coloring.

Shallot Tarte Tatin

*T*HIS IS A very elegant little tart, simultaneously sweet and savory, which you can serve warm or at room temperature. It's based on the traditional apple tart tatin, so the method will seem a little upside-down—you sauté the shallots for a while first, then put the pastry over the top, bake it, and invert it. By the end, the shallots look like deep topaz-colored jewels. It's perfect on its own, but you can serve it with a bit of sour cream and it's pure heaven.

5 tablespoons unsalted butter

5 tablespoons granulated sugar

25 shallots, peeled (see page 28)

1 tablespoon balsamic vinegar

2 sprigs thyme

1 teaspoon sea salt

1 sheet prepared pie crust dough, thawed if frozen

1. Preheat the oven to 375°F. Prep an 8-inch square cake pan by smearing it with 2 tablespoons of the butter, concentrating mostly on the bottom, then sprinkle 2 tablespoons of the sugar evenly over the bottom. Set the pan aside.

2. Melt the remaining 3 tablespoons of butter in a large skillet over medium heat and add the whole shallots. Turn them a few times in the fat, then sprinkle the remaining 3 tablespoons of sugar over the shallots.

3. Cook for 15 minutes, shaking the pan from time to time; the shallots should start to turn brown. At this point, add the balsamic vinegar, thyme, and salt. Continue cooking, watching that the sugar doesn't burn, for another 10 to 15 minutes, or until the shallots take on a deep, rich, caramel color.

4. Remove the pan from the heat and arrange cooked shallots over the bottom of the prepared baking pan, making sure that they're in a single layer. Unroll the pastry sheet, and lay it on top of the shallots, tucking it down inside the pan at the edges, like a blanket. Slide the pan into the oven and bake until the pastry is golden, 30 to 35 minutes.

5. When you take the pan out of the oven, immediately place a cutting board across the top, and say a little prayer. Quickly flip the pan over, and the shallot tarte

tatin should pop out all in one piece. If not, encourage it to fall out by nudging it with a narrow spatula or a dinner knife. Let it cool and serve it bottom side up, warm or at room temperature.

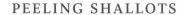

TIME: *About an hour, half unattended*
FEEDS: *4 as a starter, 2 as a main course*
SPECIAL EQUIPMENT: *The easiest way to bake this is in an 8-inch square cake pan. I prefer glass because, though the caramelization takes a little longer, you can keep track of it better.*

PEELING SHALLOTS

I OFTEN MOAN and groan when faced with a pile of onions or shallots to peel— not as much as JS does, who can tear up at a peeling onion from fifty paces—but peeling shallots is not nearly the pain in the neck that peeling garlic cloves can be. Merely chop off the top and tail of each shallot, slice through one layer to release the peel, and flip the denuded shallot into a bowl. You are now a shallot efficiency expert.

UNPEELED

CUT THE TOP & ROOT END
OFF, THEN CUT THROUGH
THE SKIN AND ONE LAYER

PEELED

Pork Chops Milanese

ONE OF MY favorite highbrow treats is veal Milanese, which involves pounding a very expensive veal chop into a pizza-size round, breading it, and frying it. One of my favorite lowbrow treats is a Japanese dish called tonkatsu, which is a less-expensive pork chop pounded thin to the size of a dinner plate, breaded, and fried. It's not the sort of thing you should eat every day, but boy, is it a treat. Here, instead of the traditional arugula salad, top the breaded pork chops with a green apple and celery root slaw. Yum.

2 rib pork chops, each one rib thick

1 large egg

¼ cup unseasoned bread crumbs

3 tablespoons freshly grated Parmesan cheese

½ teaspoon kosher salt

3 tablespoons vegetable oil

1. About an hour before you want to eat, it's time to pound and bread the pork chops. Lay a piece of parchment paper on your counter and grab yourself a meat pounder or weighty glass jar-I like to use my bottle of olive oil for this particular job. Take a sharp knife and trim away the fat rind on the chop, around the circle of meat and down onto the bone, which will serve as a sort of handle. You should have a big P going here. Now, take out your frustrations on your dinner: Using your chosen pounding tool, flatten out the pork chop, making sure to include the meat closest to the bone, until the meat is quite thin—about ⅓-inch thick. Repeat the cathartic experience with the other pork chop. Trim off any untidy bits and set the chops aside.

2. Set up the breading assembly line: Mix the egg with a drop or two of water in a shallow soup plate, then mix the bread crumbs with the Parm and the salt on a dinner plate. Finally, on another dinner plate, make a resting place for your breaded chop by laying out a piece of waxed or parchment paper. Then dip the chops in the egg, and dredge in the bread crumbs, making sure to coat each chop thoroughly. Cover the chops with another piece of waxed paper and put them in the fridge for an hour to allow the breading to set.

3. Over medium heat, heat the vegetable oil in a large skillet (preferably nonstick) with a lid for a minute, then add the pork chops, arranging them so they're not overlapping. Cook, keeping the heat modest, until golden brown on one side, about 6 minutes. Turn the chops, and cook for 8 minutes more, covering the pan at the 4-minute mark. At the end of 8 minutes, using a meat thermometer, check the internal temperature of the pork in the bit closest to the bone, which will be the thickest part—if it's more than 140°F, you're golden. If it's not, continue cooking another minute or two, and recheck the temp. Fish the chops out, place them on dinner plates, and top each with a heaping tower of the Apple and Celery Root Salad (recipe follows).

TIME: *15 minutes of cooking time, plus an hour or so of waiting around*
FEEDS: *2 birthday celebrators*

SUBSTITUTIONS AND SIMPLIFICATIONS

*S*OMETIMES YOUR BIRTHDAY wishes might not include washing fifteen pots and pans after you've had a few glasses of champagne (or Kir Royales, as you prefer). So in the interest of birthday harmony, I recommend a few cheats:

For the first course: Any savory tart works here—if you have a bakery or deli that you particularly trust, think about saving all your effort for the main course and shopping for a quiche that hits a similar note, such as onion or leek. If pork isn't your thing, you can get a similar effect with a well-pounded chicken breast; the very easy apple and celery root salad will go just as well with chicken as with pork. As for the cake—well, I think I've already made my case for homemade. But it's up to you—the most important thing is to enjoy yourself.

Apple and Celery Root Salad

CELERY ROOT—OTHERWISE known as celeriac—looks like something the Weird Sisters included in their potion for Macbeth but, despite its scary appearance, once peeled, its taste is clean and light, with an earthy tang.

½ Granny Smith apple, cored but not peeled

½ medium-size celery root, peeled

Juice of ½ lemon

A handful of parsley leaves, washed

Sea salt

1. Here's a job for that shredding blade you never use on your $100 food processor, or the julienne option on your $10 plastic mandoline, or the standard grater side of your $2 box grater. Run the apple, then the celery root, through whatever device you're using, to make a slaw.

2. Add the lemon juice, parsley leaves, and a good pinch of salt. Even with the lemon juice, this salad will turn brown pretty quickly, so make this right before you serve the pork chops, optimally while they're cooking. Of course, it's also great all by itself.

TIME: *Less than 5 minutes, including getting the parsley out of the crisper drawer*

FEEDS: *2, but easily increased*

SPECIAL EQUIPMENT: *Either a food processor or a mandoline makes this a 2-minute salad.*

Carrot Cakelettes with Lemon Icing

*T*HE TRICK IN this cake is the addition of crushed pineapple, which keeps the cake very moist and adds an exotic sweetness (thanks for the tip, Aunt Debbie). This is also not one of those carrot cakes where you'll find grated carrots—these carrots are pureed, so the cake batter is quite smooth, dotted with tiny chunks of nuts, candied ginger, and raisins. The icing is much thinner than traditional cream cheese icing, which would overwhelm the delicate cakes.

FOR THE CAKELETTES:

2 medium-size carrots, peeled and cut into large pieces

1/2 cup canned crushed pineapple with juice

1/4 cup unbleached all-purpose flour

Pinch of salt

1/2 teaspoon baking soda

1/2 teaspoon ground cinnamon

Pinch of grated nutmeg

Pinch of ground cloves

1/4 cup vegetable oil

1/4 cup light brown sugar, packed

1/4 cup granulated sugar

1 large egg

1/4 teaspoon vanilla extract

1/4 cup chopped pecans, toasted

1/4 cup chopped raw walnuts

1/4 cup golden raisins

1/4 cup chopped candied ginger

FOR THE ICING:

4 ounces cream cheese, at room temperature

Zest and juice of 2 lemons

1 tablespoon heavy cream

2/3 cup confectioners' sugar

1. To make the cakelettes: Heat 2 cups of water in a small saucepan and, when it's boiling, drop in the carrots. Cover the pan and cook the carrots over moderate heat until they are very tender, about 15 minutes. Drain.
2. Preheat the oven to 350°F. Fork the cooked carrots into a blender and then add the crushed pineapple with the juice. Give the mixture a good whiz, until uniform and gloopy (Aunt Debbie's word).
3. Lay out a large piece of waxed paper and grab your flour sifter. Sift the flour together with the salt, baking soda, and spices onto the waxed paper. Set aside.
4. In a large bowl, mix the carrot puree with the oil, brown sugar, granulated sugar

and egg until smooth. Add the flour mixture all at once and stir with a wooden spoon until just mixed. Then fold in the remaining cakelette ingredients. The batter should be nice and lumpy with the goodies you have just added.

5. Spray the muffin cups with nonstick spray, or give them a good swipe with a bit of butter wrapper, then lightly flour by knocking around a bit of flour inside them and then dumping the excess into the trash can. Fill each cup about half full with the cake batter and give the whole pan a good rap on the kitchen counter to rid the cakelettes of any air bubbles. Bake them for 20 minutes, or until a toothpick inserted into the middle of a cakelette comes out clean.

6. While the cakes are baking, make the icing: In a small bowl, smush the cream cheese around with a rubber spatula to loosen it up. Then add the lemon juice and heavy cream, mixing until uniform. Finally, add the confectioners' sugar and mix thoroughly. The icing should be thick but still pourable.

7. When the cakes are done, turn them out onto a cooling rack. The bottom of each cupcake is the top of your cakelette, so you have a perfectly smooth surface for the icing. After they cool for 30 minutes, ice the cakelettes, letting the icing drip down the sides, then let them chill out in the fridge for at least an hour before serving, birthday candle optional.

TIME: *Less than an hour*
FEEDS: *6 little cakes . . . 2 happy people*
SPECIAL EQUIPMENT: *A 6-cup muffin tin or six 6-ounce ramekins*

Kir Royale

*T*HIS IS A very traditional champagne cocktail, very belle époque. You need to get your hands on some crème de cassis, a liqueur that is available at your local booze depot. A little goes a long way, but it keeps forever so you can pull it out when you're feeling, well, celebratory. If you'd prefer to keep the imbibing moderate, look to buy a split of champagne—both cute and economical. If you're not drinking at all, a Kir Royale look-alike that will be sure to get a laugh is the Shirley Temple, beloved of seven-year-olds and designated drivers everywhere: just a splash of maraschino cherry juice in your ginger ale, and you're good to go.

Crème de cassis   Bottle of champagne

1. Pour a thimbleful of crème de cassis in the bottom of a champagne flute, then slowly pour champagne over the cassis, tilting the flute a bit to avoid accidentally fizzing over. Give a toast and drink up.

TIME: *It depends how scared you are of opening the bottle of champagne. The trick? Twist the cork out slowly, don't push it out with your thumb.*
QUENCHES: *With a split, 2; a full bottle, 6*

Flower Power
ROSES

YOU CAN SPEND many, many dollars on exotic roses and they're absolutely beautiful, and if they're a personal favorite, by all means, splurge. But if we're talking those hothouse wall-flowers you can buy in the supermarket, they need a bit of professional help. My suggestion? Sorting the grocery-store roses by color, cut their stems very short and bunch them in small glasses (old juice glasses or vintage cocktail jiggers make excellent substitutions). The water should be quite warm—this will help the roses open, which is much more attractive. It's important to make them look relaxed and a bit haphazard—the worst thing that can happen is to make them look too precious.

— A ROSE —

Birthday Cards, Third Grade-Style

✄

REMEMBER ALL THOSE presents you made out of felt, macaroni, and Elmer's glue that you gave to your mother? That glasses case? That bookmark? This is the level of crafty talent you need to make homemade birthday cards, a perfect accompaniment to the pile of presents the birthday boy or girl has to open. Hallmark is so passé, and who needs an envelope?

ARTISTIC TALENT METER: LOW

YOU'LL NEED:

Construction paper

This week's trashy tabloid or celebrity magazine

A glue stick

Scissors (use safety scissors for that real third grade vibe)

Felt-tip pens

1. First, create a card by folding a piece of construction paper in half. Very good. Then flip through the celebrity magazines, find a particularly excellent image of one of today's great personalities. (If I had to choose, I would pick Britney Spears. Even better? Celebrity mug shots.) Cut out this image and glue-stick it to the front of your card.

2. Cut a thought bubble or speech bubble out of another piece of construction paper, and glue that near the celeb's mouth. Give the celeb something to say, birthday-wise, then cut away the excess construction paper so you have the silhouette of the picture.

3. Write your heartfelt message inside, and voilà! A birthday card for the ages.

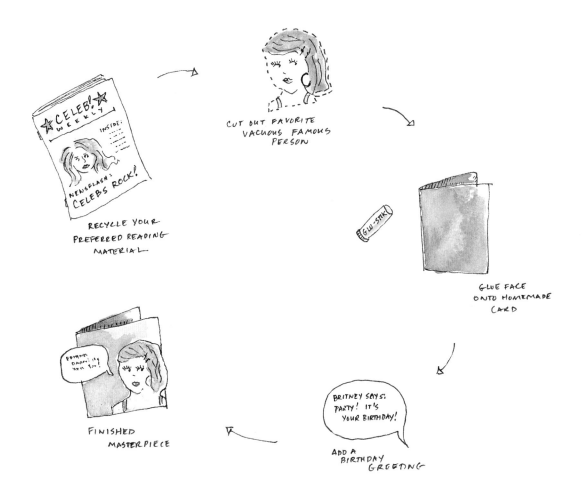

Pajama Gourmet

Real Brewed Tea (page 39)
Toasted Brioche with Golden Raisins (page 40)
Honey-Lemon Butter (page 43)
Braised Eggs with Chives and Tomato (page 44)
Brown Sugar Breakfast Sausage (page 47)
Grapefruit-Mint Fizz (page 50)

In New York, eating brunch on a Sunday means standing on line for forty minutes at some restaurant you'd never go to at any other time of day, in order to eat last night's hollandaise sauce over tepid poached eggs. You might sense from my tone that I have never been a big fan of this particular Sunday tradition, and prefer to make breakfast myself. After all, eleven thirty Sunday morning is perfect for puttering around the kitchen, eating in your pj's while you consider what to do with your last afternoon of freedom before you must return to work the next day.

The best thing about creating your own brunch spread is getting to pick and choose between sweet dishes and savory ones. Ideally, they should complement each other, the sweet having a bit of tang and the savory a touch of caramel. Toasted Brioche with Golden Raisins fills the bill- lightly sweet, particularly with the honey butter, the brioche is excellent with the sausage patties, which have just a hint of brown sugar in them.

Real Brewed Tea

$\mathcal{T}$HOUGH CHEAPO TEA bags are as much a part of my life as anyone else's, a proper English-style pot of tea is a joy to drink and is much more satisfying than is the astringent taste of over-steeped orange pekoe. Brew up a pot, and you'll feel like Charlotte Brontë or Jane Austen, except with better teeth and hair.

1 tablespoon good-quality loose black tea-
   Darjeeling or English Breakfast

½ cup whole milk

A few thin slices of lemon

Granulated sugar

1. Bring at least a quart of cold water to a boil in a teakettle. Rinse out your dusty teapot, and, when the kettle is whistling, pour a cup or so of water in your teapot and give it a swirl. Let it sit for a minute—this allows the pot to heat up—and then pour the water out. Place the tea leaves in the pot, pour 3 cups of boiling water over the leaves, put the top on the teapot and let the tea steep for 5 minutes.
2. Meanwhile, set up a tea tray—in my house, a haphazard collection of teacups and saucers, a creamer, a small plate for the lemon slices, and a sugar bowl with a long ago broken lid. You'll also need a small strainer to pour the tea through. Warm the milk in the microwave until just tepid, probably 30 seconds but it depends on your machine. Pour the milk into the creamer, place a bit of sugar in the sugar bowl, and set out a few teaspoons.
3. Pour the steeped tea, making sure to strain it so that the leaves don't migrate to your tea cup. Add sugar, and milk or lemon as you prefer.

TIME: *About 10 minutes, for water-boiling purposes*
QUENCHES: *2*
SPECIAL EQUIPMENT: *A little fine-mesh strainer for the tea—these are widely available and not very expensive, and they also double well as a way to strain pips out of lemon or orange juice.*

Toasted Brioche with Golden Raisins

I KNOW MAKING bread sounds like a scary process—I mean, there's yeast involved—but it's really not. It's fun. Remember how much fun Play-Doh was? Well, this is similar, but tastes better. Brioche is wonderfully eggy and light, with a subtle sweetness and a soft crust. It's important to plan ahead and make the dough the afternoon before—it needs time to rise. You can also make the dough well ahead and freeze it—just let it defrost in the refrigerator the night before you want it.

1/3 cup lukewarm whole or 2% milk (heated so it is slightly warm to the touch)

1 (1/4 ounce) package active dry yeast (not rapid rise)

5 large eggs, at room temperature

1/3 cup sugar, plus an extra pinch

1 1/2 cups unbleached all-purpose flour

1 teaspoon kosher salt

2 cups bread flour (see note)

1 1/2 sticks unsalted butter, cubed, softened

2/3 cup golden raisins, soaked in 1/2 cup hot water for 5 minutes and drained

1/4 cup heavy cream

1. The day before, make the sponge (the yeast base of the brioche): Mix the warm milk with the yeast, 1 egg, a pinch of sugar, and 1 cup of the all-purpose flour in the bowl of your mixer until just combined, then sprinkle the remaining 1/2 cup of all-purpose flour over the yeast mixture and let it sit in a warm place to develop, between 30 minutes and an hour. When the dusting of flour on the top of the sponge looks cracked, it's ready.

2. Add the remaining 4 eggs, the 1/3 cup of sugar, the kosher salt, and 1 cup of the bread flour, and give it a slow mix for about 2 minutes, until the dough comes together. Slowly sprinkle in the second cup of bread flour. Once the flour is incorporated, turn the mixer up a notch and let it run, scraping down the sides of the bowl from time to time, until the dough clings to the dough hook but isn't pasting itself to the sides of the bowl, about 15 minutes.

3. At this point, add the softened butter, small piece by small piece, until it's com-

pletely incorporated. Keep mixing the dough for 5 more minutes. In the last moments, add the drained golden raisins, mixing until they're evenly distributed. The dough will feel very sticky and soft, but will look quite shiny and beautiful.

4. Cover the mixing bowl with plastic wrap and let the dough rise in a warm room for 2 to 3 hours, until it has doubled in volume. Gently deflate the dough with your fist, re-cover with the old plastic wrap, and stick it in the fridge overnight.

5. First thing in the morning, butter two standard loaf pans (I like Pyrex glass ones so you can see how brown the bottom is getting). Take the dough out of the fridge, scrape it out onto a cutting board (a little flour might be called for here), and divide the dough in half, and then into thirds, so you have six pieces. Form each piece into a loose ball, then tuck three of them into each of the prepared pans. Let them stand on the counter for an hour.

6. Preheat the oven to 375°F. Brush the tops of the loaves lightly with the heavy cream, then pop them in the oven. Bake for 30 minutes.

7. For the toast: cut hearty slices-at least 1½ inch thick-and toast them until golden, spreading the toast with the Honey-Lemon Butter (page 43).

⁓

TIME: *Several hours on the day before you want to serve the brioche, mostly unattended, and an hour of rising and baking time the day of*
FEEDS: *This makes 2 loaves, 1 for breakfast today and 1 frozen for another breakfast, within 2 months*
SPECIAL EQUIPMENT: *You can (and should) use a standing mixer with a dough hook if you have one, but a mixer is absolutely not necessary. It's only a slight workout to knead by hand. Instead of the 15 minutes in the machine, it's 15 minutes on a well-floured board or counter surface.*
NOTE: *This recipe calls for bread flour, which gives the brioche a heartier texture, particularly nice at breakfast time. A great mail-order source is www.kingarthur.com. Its catalog is a smorgasbord of baking supplies. If that's too much bother, use unbleached all-purpose flour instead.*

My Secret Shame: Coffee

I'm scared of espresso machines. I don't know how to use them (I've never been a barista), and if I need one, well, there are only a few thousand coffeehouses in the five square blocks around my apartment.

So this is the one cooking task assigned to JS: he makes the coffee. His weapon of choice? The French press, the easiest of all coffeemakers. It won't hiss and spit at you as an espresso maker will, and it costs way less. All you need to do is spoon a tablespoon of grounds per cup into the bottom of the press, add boiling water, and attach the cap. After a few minutes of steeping, press the plunger down, and pour. An extra bonus is that it looks very cute on a breakfast or dinner table.

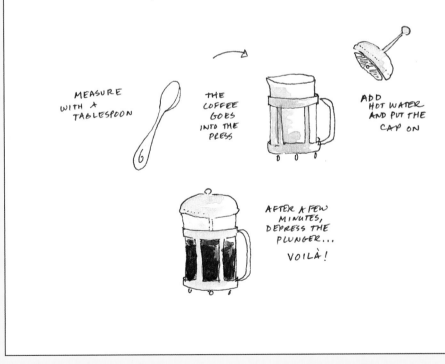

MEASURE WITH A TABLESPOON

THE COFFEE GOES INTO THE PRESS

ADD HOT WATER AND PUT THE CAP ON

AFTER A FEW MINUTES, DEPRESS THE PLUNGER...

VOILÀ!

Honey-Lemon Butter

$\mathcal{M}$AKE THIS WHEN you make the dough for the brioche, and stick it in the freezer so it's ready to go the next day. It will keep in the freezer for months, and is just as good on English muffins, pancakes, or waffles—even freezer-burned Eggos, as JS will attest.

¼ pound (1 stick) unsalted butter, softened	Zest of ½ lemon
3 tablespoons honey	1 tablespoon freshly squeezed lemon juice

1. In a small bowl, whack the softened butter with a rubber spatula a few times, until it is spread out and any lumps are gone.
2. In another bowl, mix the honey with the lemon zest and juice, then scrape and fold that mixture into the beaten butter, working it until everything is nice and smooth.
3. Spread out a piece of waxed paper or plastic wrap, and then mound the flavored butter in the middle. Wrap up the butter, then mold it into a little log as best you can. My logs always look a bit homely, but don't sweat it. Throw it in the refrigerator at least an hour before serving.

TIME: *Mere moments, as long as the butter is softened*
FEEDS: *Makes enough for 8 servings, if you're restrained with butter application*

Braised Eggs with Chives and Tomato

THIS IS A stovetop dish, best made in the summer with really, really ripe tomatoes, or in the winter with the absolute best quality Italian canned tomatoes you can find. The only difference between the two is that you should cook the canned tomatoes a bit longer before you add the eggs—about five minutes should do it.

2 large, very ripe fresh tomatoes, or 2½ cups whole canned plum tomatoes, drained

1 tablespoon olive oil

2 scallions, sliced thinly, white and light green parts only

½ teaspoon kosher salt

2 teaspoons red wine vinegar

Freshly ground pepper

A bunch of fresh chives

4 large eggs

1. If you're using fresh tomatoes: bring a pot of water to a boil, then drop in the tomatoes, letting them blanch for 30 seconds or so. Remove them with a slotted spoon or bamboo-handled strainer, then let them sit for a second (out of sympathy for your fingers) until they cool slightly. Use a paring knife to make a quick incision on the bottom of each tomato, and peel the skin away with your fingers. Cut the tomatoes in half horizontally, and gently squeeze each half above the trash can or disposal to rid yourself of as many seeds as possible. Give the tomatoes a rough chop and set aside. If you're using canned tomatoes, give them a rough chop and set aside.

2. Heat the oil in a large, preferably nonstick skillet, over medium-high heat until it shimmers but isn't smoking. Add the scallions and turn them in the oil until you can smell them, just 30 seconds. Add the tomatoes, give the mixture a stir, and then add the salt, the vinegar, and several grindings of pepper. Lower the heat and cook, stirring once or twice, for 8 minutes. If you're using canned tomatoes, give them another 5. The tomatoes should just be softening and giving up their juice. They shouldn't be total mush. Taste for seasoning, then snip chives over the top of the sauce with your kitchen scissors, being as generous as you like.

3. Turn up the heat to medium-high, then make four little wells in the tomato sauce with the back of a wooden spoon. Carefully crack the eggs, one by one, into the pan, aiming for each well. Reduce the heat to medium, and cook until the egg whites are completely solidified and the yolks turn opaque, 4 to 5 minutes. (It can be useful to cover the pan for a minute or two of that time). Top with a few more snipped chives, and serve immediately.

TIME: *About 15 minutes*
FEEDS: *2 breakfasters*
SPECIAL EQUIPMENT: *A nonstick pan*

Brunching It Up

*W*HEN, AS SOMETIMES happens to me, your brother shows up unannounced at your door early Sunday afternoon, and you have to augment the nice breakfast you've made for two, this is how you do it:

For loose tea, add a teaspoon of tea leaves and a cup of water per person. And there's always a teaspoon for the pot.

There's plenty of brioche, if you defrost the second loaf. In fact, there's enough for eight in the two loaves.

The eggs are a bit tricky—you can add another two eggs to the pan with the tomato sauce as it is, but if you need to make more, double the tomato recipe and make the eggs in two pans. The surface area is important here.

The sausage recipe and the grapefruit fizz recipe are easily doubled, or tripled, or quadrupled. You catch my drift.

MEASURING FLOUR

*T*HE TRICK IS to spoon the flour into the measuring cup, not use the measuring cup as a scoop, which packs down the flour and gives you more than you need. When the measuring cup is filled, use the back of a knife to gently distribute the flour, then remove the excess with an expert flick.

USE A WOODEN SPOON TO FILL YOUR MEASURING CUP...

...AND A DINNER KNIFE TO EASE OFF THE EXCESS..

Brown Sugar Breakfast Sausage

INTRODUCING THIS RECIPE is just asking for trouble. I mean, how's a girl supposed to say with a straight face that she loves sausage? The fact is, I do, but I'm very picky. For breakfast, I'm a patty girl, rather than a links girl, but so many premade patties are tough and rubbery. Not these.

1 tablespoon olive oil

½ small onion, chopped finely

1 teaspoon fresh rosemary, chopped finely, or a pinch of dried rosemary

1 tablespoon dark brown sugar

½ pound breakfast sausage (the kind froz in a tube is perfect here)

2 tablespoons vegetable oil

1. In a nonstick pan that will subsequently be used for the patties, sauté the onion in the olive oil for 3 minutes, until translucent. Scrape the onions into a small mixing bowl and let them cool for 5 minutes or so.
2. Add the rosemary and brown sugar, to the onions, then the breakfast sausage, and smush the mixture between your fingers until it's blended. Don't worry about salt—there's already plenty in the sausage. Form the mixture into six little patties.
3. Heat the vegetable oil in the pan, then add the sausage patties, and cook until golden brown on both sides, about 6 minutes total.

TIME: *15 minutes*

FEEDS: *Well, 2, technically, though I can eat 6 of the best sausage patties at one sitting, can't you?*

Egg Centerpieces

WHEN YOU'RE HAVING a special-occasion brunch—celebrating Easter, or baseball opening day, or a new pair of boots, or something—your standard Sunday morning table decor of unwashed wineglasses from the night before might be a bit lacking. So try this inexpensive and fun centerpiece.

Eggs are beautiful and elegant, and once you empty them of their yolks and whites, the shells can stay in a bowl for as long as you like. I'm using brown chicken eggs, easily found at the supermarket—look for a dozen with subtle variations of color—but if you can get your hands on other eggs (I've used quail eggs and even partridge eggs I bought at the farmers' market) they'll make a striking and unusual centerpiece as well.

You can arrange these eggs on a shallow oval platter, or in wire baskets, in small footed bowls, or even old-fashioned eggcups. The eggs just have to be secure.

ARTISTIC TALENT METER: LOW

YOU NEED:

> A dozen brown eggs
>
> A thumbtack
>
> Sharpened pencils
>
> Crayons
>
> Scissors
>
> An old brown paper bag

1. Take an egg and, gently but firmly, poke a hole in each end of the egg with the thumbtack, wiggling the tack in each puncture so that you make sure the interior membrane is broken. Now, discover your inner Louis Armstrong and blow into

the egg (naturally, over the sink or into a bowl), keeping the pressure steady. The egg white and yolk will come flying out the other side. Give the emptied egg a rinse, then wipe it dry with a kitchen towel. Rest the egg in the egg carton, and continue until you've cleared out all the eggs.

2. Sometimes, if I have some spare time, I decorate the eggs with little drawings or caricatures. See the sketches for some ideas.

3. Make the nesting material: pleat the old paper bag as if you were making a fan, creasing it firmly. Cut the bag into thin (about ¼-inch) strips, aiming your scissors perpendicularly to the pleats, so that each strip is crinkled. You can use this in the bottom of your platter or basket as nesting material. I like the simplicity of the brown paper, but whatever you want to use, you can. I sometimes use bunches of chives for a burst of color, but of course that's not a long-lasting option.

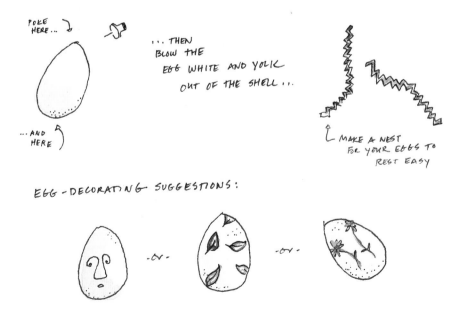

POKE HERE...

...AND HERE

...THEN BLOW THE EGG WHITE AND YOLK OUT OF THE SHELL...

MAKE A NEST FOR YOUR EGGS TO REST EASY

EGG-DECORATING SUGGESTIONS:

-or-

-or-

Grapefruit-Mint Fizz

$\mathcal{M}$Y FATHER HAS always had an orange juice ritual—for Christmas, my Aunt Pat sends him special juicing oranges from Florida, and he squeezes them in his old-fashioned juicer, pressing them one at a time. That's some good orange juice. Freshly squeezed is always better, isn't it? Here, I'm using my favorite citrus, the good old ruby red grapefruit—it has an astringent, refreshing taste and a beautiful blush color, and the seltzer's bubbles play up the tartness.

2 ruby red grapefruits, juiced

2 cups seltzer or club soda

2 teaspoons superfine sugar (or to taste)

2 small sprigs fresh mint

1. Mix the grapefruit juice, seltzer, and sugar in a pitcher and stir until the sugar is dissolved. Place a few ice cubes and the mint sprigs into two glasses, and pour the fizz over the top.

TIME: *About 5 minutes*

QUENCHES: *2*

NICE THINGS TO HAVE AT A WEEKEND BREAKFAST

LOCAL TABLOID

10-POUND FASHION BIBLE

SUNDAY CROSSWORD

METS GAME ON THE TUBE

BOSSA NOVA

Late-Nite Dishing

MENU 1: PLANNING AHEAD
Chicken Curry Potpies (page 52)
Celery Salad with Spicy Goat Cheese (page 56)

MENU 2: BY THE SEAT OF YOUR PANTS
Side-Dish Frittata (page 58)
Simple Chickpea Salad (page 60)

AND FOR DESSERT:
Cinnamon-Vanilla Smoothies (page 62)

It always feels a little naughty to have dinner at midnight. To me it reminds me of raiding the dining hall fridge at sleepaway camp, and the food always tastes the better for the excitement. Sometimes you'll eat very well late at night— after the theater, or a cocktail party, for instance, when you're still dressed up and happy to rehash your evening at length. Those are the moments when you can plan ahead, and have a tasty dinner ready to go with little muss and fuss.

Sometimes, however, it's more a question of: Where did the night go? And, Geez, I'm starving, what's in the refrigerator? In these instances, though JS often opts for five bowls of Cap'n Crunch, sometimes you need a bit more than children's cereal and the *Daily Show* on TV to get by. That's when you make do with some pantry staples and whip up a dinner in less than twenty minutes.

Finally, there's no fun eating late if you're not going to eat something bad. Every girl knows that calories consumed after midnight don't count, so why not treat yourself to a cinnamon smoothie? You probably won't regret it in the morning.

Chicken Curry Potpies

*T*HERE'S A KITCHEN appliance you can buy for less than $20 that will make you a better-adjusted person. So fire your shrink, and buy a toaster oven. Sure, you can use your conventional oven for this late-night treat, but it's way more midnight-snacky to use your toaster oven.

The potpie itself makes a perfect one-dish late-night treat: it's homey and classic, and the flavors aren't complicated or provoking. It's a neat package of pastry and creamy sauce that makes for a satisfying supper.

TO POACH THE CHICKEN:

1 chicken breast, on the bone

A few sprigs parsley

A few sprigs cilantro

5 peppercorns

A bay leaf

1 teaspoon kosher salt

FOR THE POTPIE FILLING:

2 tablespoons unsalted butter

2 tablespoons all-purpose flour

1 cup chicken stock, hot, or 1 cup boiling water in which a bouillon cube has been dissolved

1 cup coconut milk

1 tablespoon red curry paste

1 teaspoon good-quality curry powder

½ teaspoon kosher salt

½ red onion, sliced into hearty half-moons

1 small sweet potato, peeled and cubed

½ cup frozen peas

¼ cup chopped fresh parsley

¼ cup chopped cilantro

FOR THE CRUST:

1 sheet of prepared pie dough, thawed and unrolled

1 egg, lightly beaten

1. Poach the chicken: Put the chicken breast, parsley and cilantro, peppercorns, bay leaf, and kosher salt in a saucepan full of cold water and bring to a boil over high heat. As soon as you see rapid bubbles, reduce the heat to low and simmer the chicken gently for 20 minutes. If you're concerned about doneness, the best way to check is a meat thermometer, which should read 160°F when you stick it into the thickest part of the breast. Drain the breast and set it aside to cool off a bit.

2. Start the filling: In a medium-size saucepan, melt the butter over lively heat, then add the flour and stir with a wooden spoon to press out any lumps and cook the flour a bit. Slowly add the chicken stock—keep on stirring, or things will get

THE TWO OF US . . . AND FRIENDS

a bit lumpy—and then the coconut milk. Add the curry paste, the curry powder, and the ½ teaspoon of salt—taste to test saltiness.

3. Add the onions and the sweet potato to the saucepan, lower the heat to a simmer, and let the veggies cook for 6 to 8 minutes, or until your cubes of sweet potato are tender. While the vegetables are simmering, pull the bones and skin away from the chicken breast and cut the meat into 1-inch pieces. When the sweet potato is cooked, add the chicken to the pot, along with the frozen peas and the chopped herbs. Give everything a good turn in the sauce. Turn off the heat and set the saucepan aside.

4. Use this high-tech method to create the pastry tops for the potpies: Cut the pastry sheet into quarters, then put a ramekin on top of each quarter and trim off the excess pastry dough around them, leaving yourself ½ inch grace.

5. Fill each ramekin to the brim with the chicken stew. Moisten the lip of the ramekins, and top each with a pastry round, pressing down on the edges with the tines of a fork. Paint the tops of the pastry rounds with the egg wash, and cut a small steam vent or two in the center. You can now stick these in the fridge until you need them (see note).

6. Now for the toaster oven: Preheat to 200°F. Cover the tops of the potpies with foil, and bake for 10 minutes. Remove the foil and let the pastry brown, another 5 to 8 minutes. Be careful when turning up the heat or the tops will burn before the insides are heated through. If you must bake these in the conventional oven, preheat it to 325°F, place them on a rimmed cookie sheet, eschew the foil, and bake them for 15 to 20 minutes.

TIME: *Less than an hour*
FEEDS: *This recipe makes 4, so you four times, or 2 people, twice.*
SPECIAL EQUIPMENT: *Four 8-ounce ramekins*
NOTE: *The point of these is to make them ahead, either earlier in the day, or (more likely) well in advance, so they're sitting in the freezer until you need them, securely wrapped in aluminum foil. If that's the case, let your potpies defrost in the refrigerator for at least several hours before you go out, then cook in the same way as I've detailed here, giving them 5 more minutes for good measure.*

Oh my beautiful toaster oven! If I were even the least bit poetically inclined, I would write an ode to it. But as I'm not, I'll merely illustrate what miracles you can cook up with a little creativity and a toaster oven:

MOST EXCELLENT TUNA MELTS: Toast some rye bread, then top with tuna fish salad and a thin slice of sharp Cheddar cheese. Broil away, until the cheese is bubbling. A glass of water with a slice of lemon, and an Oreo cookie or two, and you've got a great supper.

LATE-NITE CROQUE MONSIEUR: Top a slice of white bread (day-old country bread is perfectly acceptable) with a slather of whole-grain mustard, a slice of whatever ham you have handy, and some shredded Swiss cheese. Bake at 250°F until golden. If you have any prewashed salad around, toss a handful with a squeeze of lemon, some sea salt, and the barest hint of oil for a quick side salad. Plate it, then pour yourself a glass of red and enjoy.

TINY PEACH TARTS: For a bit of freshness after a late-nite take-out meal, cut the crusts off a slice of white sandwich bread, then flatten it with your palm. Butter the bread, then arrange a few slices of fresh peach on top, along with several teaspoons of sugar out of your sugar bowl and a pinch of cinnamon. Bake at 250°F until the edges are golden and the peaches have relaxed a bit, about 15 minutes.

SALT-BAKED POTATO: Pour ½ cup of coarse sea salt on the baking tray of your toaster oven, and bury a rosemary sprig in the middle. Scrub an Idaho potato, then prick it all over with the tip of a knife. Bake at 300°F, turning once, until tender, about 50 minutes. Serve with lots of butter, pepper, and a squeeze of lemon. To make this a meal, add a sliver or two of thinly sliced prosciutto on top and pop open a beer.

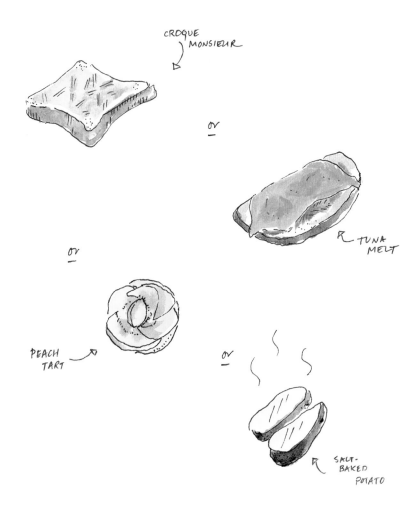

CROQUE
MONSIEUR

or

TUNA
MELT

or

PEACH
TART

or

SALT-
BAKED
POTATO

Celery Salad with Spicy Goat Cheese

A TERRIFIC AND unusual five-minute salad.

¼ cup soft, plain goat cheese	1 tablespoon olive oil
¼ teaspoon red pepper flakes, crushed	Juice of ½ lemon
1 head of celery	Sea salt

1. In a small bowl, mix the goat cheese with the crushed red pepper flakes. Set aside.
2. Snap the darker outer stalks away from the head of celery; all you want here are the stalks that go from pale green into chartreuse. Separate and give them a good wash. Slice on the diagnol into lovely long U's and save the innermost leaves to put in the salad as well.
3. Throw the celery and the celery leaves into a serving bowl, and add the olive oil, lemon juice, and sea salt, to taste. Dot the top of the salad with the spicy goat cheese, give the celery a quick turn, and the salad is ready to be eaten.

TIME: *Less than 10 minutes*
FEEDS: *2 as a side dish*

Care and Feeding of Small Appliances

They may be small, but they're scrappy, and if you treat them right, they'll treat you right.

FOR YOUR FOOD PROCESSOR:

Every time you wash the top, make sure you dismantle it to the fullest extent, and give everything a good wash—this holds true if you wash it in a dishwasher, too. Sometimes it's easy to plunk the whole thing down and give it a rinse. It looks clean, right? But without careful cleaning, the whole works will eventually get gummed up. You can wipe down the unit itself with dish soap, making sure the motor's vents are free of dust.

FOR YOUR TOASTER OVEN:

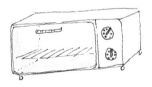

Please, empty that crumb tray! Just pull it down or out, depending on the model, and give it a good wash. I like stainless steel ones, but if you have one with a white plastic cover, and it gets a bit yellowed, you can give it a wipe with some white vinegar mixed with baking soda.

FOR YOUR BLENDER:

When you clean your blender, make sure you unscrew the blade from the glass pitcher and wash it thoroughly. A few extra seconds really getting under those blades makes it absolutely sure that your Cinnamon Smoothie doesn't taste like yesterday's basil pesto.

Side-Dish Frittata

$\mathcal{E}$GGS ARE AN absolute kitchen staple, and they've been a dinner-saver many a time, both late in the evening when you don't want to go out to pick up groceries, or on a Sunday when the New York Jets are playing and you refuse to go out and pick up groceries, lest you miss something important.

Ideally, you make this frittata with side-dish leftovers from another meal—the little pile of sautéed spinach, for instance, or the cold and shriveled roasted potatoes. Here, I manufacture the side-dish elements for you before they go into the eggs, but let this recipe (though delicious) act merely as a springboard into your own side-dish frittatas.

1/3 cup orzo	1/2 teaspoon kosher salt
2 tablespoons unsalted butter	6 eggs
2 cups Swiss chard, coarsely chopped, stems discarded, washed but not dried	1/2 cup freshly grated Parmesan cheese
1/2 cup smoked ham, cubed	Pepper
2 cups fresh spinach leaves, washed but not dried	

1. In a large nonstick skillet, the future home of the frittata, toast the orzo over medium heat for 5 minutes, stirring often, until the pasta turns golden brown. Meanwhile, bring a small pot of water to a boil, into which goes the toasted orzo. Boil for 8 minutes.

2. Meanwhile, return the skillet to the heat and melt 1 tablespoon of the butter. Add the Swiss chard, tossing it about until it collapses. Herd the greens to a corner of the pan and add the smoked ham. Let these two items cook cozily for 3 or 4 minutes, stirring every once in a while.

3. While that's going on, crack the eggs into a bowl and beat them with a tablespoon or two of water (you can eyeball this) and the Parmesan. Add a few grindings of pepper.

4. A minute before the orzo is done, add the spinach to the skillet and let

it wilt. Drain the orzo, and add it to the pan, along with the remaining tablespoon of butter. Swirl the butter through the pan, and give everything a good mix. Finally, spread everything out so that there's an even layer of goodies before you pour the eggs over them. When you pour, try to pour evenly, then tilt the pan and poke about with a spoon or spatula so that the egg binds everything together. Reduce the heat to a minimum and cover the pan, cooking for 6 to 8 minutes. The egg will cook through and puff up in a very pretty way.

5. To serve, flip the frittata over, onto a cutting board, and cut into wedges. You can eat this hot—as now—or at room temperature for lunch the next day.

TIME: *About 20 minutes*
FEEDS: *2 people very well, or four with a generous helping of salad*

MULTIPLICATION TABLE
Salads

*I*F YOU'RE INCLINED to make the celery salad for more than two, factor in a head of celery per two people, because you really want to strip away most of the more fibrous outer stalks. You can save them for making chicken stock (see page 66).

The chickpea salad has enough dressing to accommodate at least half again as many chickpeas; if you want to double the recipe, just increase the salad dressing ingredients accordingly, but keeping it to just the one egg yolk.

Simple Chickpea Salad

*T*HIS IS MODELED after a salad I love in the summertime. It's so simple, but the trick is in the smooth, tangy, foolproof dressing. For those afraid of raw eggs, you can leave the yolk out, but it really adds a perfect creaminess to the salad.

1 tablespoon Dijon mustard

1 tablespoon white wine vinegar

½ teaspoon kosher salt

Pepper

1 egg yolk (optional)

¼ cup olive oil

⅓ cup Vidalia or Spanish onion, thinly sliced

1 (15-ounce) can chickpeas, well drained and rinsed

1 tablespoon finely chopped fresh parsley (optional)

1. Grab a medium-size bowl and a fork and make the dressing: mix the mustard with the vinegar, then add the kosher salt and pepper to taste. Stir in the egg yolk. Then, mixing continuously, add the olive oil in a constant stream, until you get a wonderful, creamy, and completely uniform salad dressing (chef-types would say emulsified, which just means that the oil hasn't separated from the vinegar). Taste and correct for salt and pepper.
2. Add the onion and the chickpeas, and stir to coat. That's it—you can add the parsley if it's looking a little too beige to you.

TIME: *5 minutes*

FEEDS: *2, generously*

FLEA MARKET TABLETOP FINDS FOR UNDER $15:

I'M NOT THE first person to tell you to hie yourself to the local flea market. There are so many wonderful kitchen things to buy, and if they break, well, you haven't broken the bank. Here are a few treasures to look for:

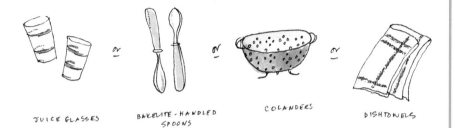

JUICE GLASSES — BAKELITE-HANDLED SPOONS — COLANDERS — DISHTOWELS

Cinnamon-Vanilla Smoothies

$\mathcal{T}$HIS SOUNDS LIKE a terrible cliché, but JS only knows how to make one thing in the kitchen: a mess. No, I kid. That thing is a vanilla milk shake, not-quite-blended in such a way that the shake separates into very cold, very sweet milk, and a lump of frostbitten ice cream in the middle.

I know, it's the thought that counts.

The honey in the recipe, along with the vanilla ice cream, mellows out the bite of the cinnamon. It's like a cinnamon-scented cloud of ice cream.

Handful of ice cubes

1 pint vanilla ice cream

1 tablespoon honey

1½ tablespoons ground cinnamon

1½ cups whole milk

1. If you have a refrigerator that coughs up crushed ice, scoop about ½ cup's worth into the pitcher of your blender. If you, like me, are not so lucky, just blend a few ice cubes into oblivion. Pry the ice cream out of its paper container and add to the blender, along with the honey and the cinnamon. Blend!

2. Through the pour spout in the blender's lid (you did remember to put the lid on the blender, didn't you?), add the milk in a steady stream. Get out two beer steins (this is the only thing I use beer steins for) or large glasses and have yourself a frosty cinnamon smoothie.

3. I should mention that, since this is liquid, these are calorie-free. I swear.

TIME: *3 minutes*

FEEDS: *2, much more than they should have at one sitting*

Party of Four

Winter Warm-Up

Garlic Soup with Croutons (page 65)
Red and Orange Beef Short Ribs (page 67)
Potatoes Roasted with Olives (page 69)
Braised Red Peppers (page 70)
Frisée and Baby Greens with Fig Dressing (page 74)
Cheese
Brown Sugar Pudding with Raspberries (page 75)

When I first started cooking for friends, and had a very limited budget, I would make them beef short ribs. Short ribs look fancier than regular old stew, and their texture—velvety soft—when complemented with their flavor—deeply beefy—makes quite an impression on dinner guests. Such depth of flavor is extremely hard to create with such little work in any other dish. As you might expect, this dinner is particularly good on a cold night, and it smells wonderful when it's cooking.

So to warm up your cooking arm, I suggest making the winter warm-up dish, Red and Orange Beef Short Ribs, the centerpiece of your menu. The beefiness is deepened by red wine and livened up by a hint of orange peel. Since the beef, even in small portions, is quite hearty, keep the dinner's other elements light but flavorful. To start, you can make a really simple but delicious soup out of nothing more than chicken broth, garlic, and day-old country bread. The braised beef is well paired with the gussied-up roasted potatoes and the smokiness of the red peppers. Finally, I'm a sucker for puddings. Homemade pudding is a snap and a crowd-pleaser nonpareil.

Garlic Soup with Croutons

*D*ON'T IMAGINE SOME dense, murky soup made out of thousands of garlic cloves. This is a wonderful, delicate soup, which is even better if the chicken broth is homemade. The best part of this soup is the crunchy, garlicky croutons. Croutons make people happy.

6 cups good-quality chicken stock, preferably homemade (see page 66)

1 teaspoon kosher salt (optional)

12 cloves of garlic, peeled and slivered
(see note)

½ cup extra-virgin olive oil

8 slices day-old baguette or country bread,
about ½-inch thick

A pinch of hot pepper flakes

3 tablespoons finely chopped fresh parsley

1. Heat the chicken stock to a simmer in a large saucepan, on a back burner. Add the kosher salt if you've made the stock yourself; otherwise, taste for saltiness and make an executive decision.

2. Meanwhile, put the olive oil and the slivered garlic in a cold skillet, then heat the pan gently, over low heat, stirring occasionally, until the garlic is lightly golden, about 8 minutes. Scoop the garlic out of the oil and into the simmering broth with a slotted spoon. Be diligent about this and try to get every little last sliver, because any remaining bit of garlic might burn and affect the taste of the the oil when it is used to toast the croutons.

3. When the oil is garlic-free, raise the heat to medium. Slip the bread slices into the oil and toast until golden on both sides, about 4 minutes. Fish the finished croutons out of the oil and set them aside on paper towels. By the time all the bread is toasted, the oil will have been completely absorbed. Finally, add the pinch of hot pepper to the stock.

4. To serve, ladle the garlic broth into shallow soup plates, then float the croutons in the middle and sprinkle with chopped parsley.

TIME: *If you have chicken stock on hand, about 20 minutes*

FEEDS: *4 as a first course, or 2 for a Sunday supper*

NOTE: *For this soup, I use those prepeeled garlic cloves you can buy in the produce aisle. I hate peeling garlic cloves and can't resist that someone else has already done this for me. Julia Child is probably rolling over in her grave at this admission, but make of it what you will.*

CHICKEN STOCK 1, 2, 3

*T*O PROVE TO you that it's not hard to make your own chicken stock, I am presenting it pictorially, the way they show you to find the emergency exits on a 767:

Red and Orange Beef Short Ribs

I MADE THESE recently, and a friend said, "This chicken is great!" I can assure you, these ribs taste nothing like chicken, but he was eating so fast that maybe the synapses connecting his mouth to his brain were disrupted. Anyway, the key word here is "great!" Capice?

8 meaty beef short ribs, trimmed

1/3 cup all-purpose flour

2 1/2 teaspoons kosher salt

4 tablespoons vegetable oil

1/3 cup pancetta, cut into matchsticks

2 medium-size carrots, peeled and finely chopped

1 medium-size onion, peeled and chopped

2 medium-size leeks, white and light green parts, washed, dried, and chopped

2 cloves garlic, peeled and smashed

1 tablespoon light molasses

1 bouquet garni: 1 sprig parsley, 1 sprig thyme, 1 bay leaf, 15 peppercorns, and 1 whole clove, tied up together in a piece of cheesecloth

1 cup beef stock (you can use a bouillon cube here)

3 1/2 cups red wine

A curl of orange peel

1. Preheat the oven to 325°F.
2. Heat a large casserole with a lid—the cast-iron, ovenproof kind is best here—over lively heat and add 2 tablespoons of the oil. While the pan is heating, mix the flour and 2 teaspoons of the kosher salt on a dinner plate, and dredge the short ribs one by one, slipping each short rib into the hot oil as soon as it has been dredged. Brown these puppies carefully, without crowding the pan—you'll probably have to do this in two batches. Set the browned short ribs aside.
3. Decant the fat in the pan into a disposable and nonmeltable container—not down your drain!—and wipe the pan free of any excess beef fat using a piece of paper towel held with tongs. Return the pot to the heat, add the remaining oil, and then the pancetta. Swirl the pancetta in the fat for 30 seconds, then throw in the vegetables and the remaining salt. Sweat the veggies for 5 minutes, until the carrots soften and the onion turns translucent. Add the molasses, and stir to coat.
4. Return the short ribs to the pan, along with the bouquet garni, beef stock, and red wine. While the liquid is slowly coming to the boil, make the pot a paper party hat—cut a circle out of parchment paper (waxed paper will melt, so don't use it) that will

fit just inside the lip of the pot. The casserole top comes in handy as a template here. When you see that the braising stock is beginning to boil, cover the short ribs with the parchment round, cover the casserole securely with its top, and slide the whole lot into the oven, where you will leave it, undisturbed, for 2½ hours.

5. After 2½ hours (suggestion: watch *The Godfather* in the meantime), pull the casserole from the oven and take a peek inside. Things should be looking rich and smelling good. The ribs themselves should be fork tender, but not mush. Throw away the parchment paper, and pick the ribs out of the sauce, throwing away any bones that fall off. Let them cool, put them in an airtight container, and stick them in the refrigerator. As for the sauce, pour it into a separate container, and add the orange peel. Refrigerate the sauce overnight.

6. An hour before you want to eat, take the short ribs and their sauce out of the fridge. The beef fat that was rendered out of the ribs will have formed a cake on top of the sauce. Amuse yourself for a minute prying it off and throwing it away. Combine the sauce—cold, it will be very gelatinous—and the short ribs in a heavy-bottomed pot, cover, and heat over minimum heat until bubbling and ready to serve. Each person gets two short ribs and many spoonfuls of the lovely sauce.

⌒

TIME: *Start this the day before you need it, for easy fat removal*
FEEDS: *4*
SPECIAL EQUIPMENT: *You'll need a length of cheesecloth, easily purchased at the supermarket.*

MULTIPLICATION TABLE
Short Ribs

IT'S WORTH MENTIONING that when you make this for eight instead of four, you don't need to directly double the liquid. In fact, for sixteen spare ribs, I would use eight cups of liquid, six of wine and two of beef stock. The most important thing is that the spare ribs are submerged when you slide the casserole into the oven. All the other ingredients can be doubled in the ordinary way.

Potatoes Roasted with Olives

THE OLIVES IN this dish are a tasty counterpoint to the faint orange flavor in the short ribs.

3 pounds Yukon Gold or white potatoes, rinsed

½ cup oil-cured black olives, pitted

½ cup green olives, such as picholines, pitted

3 tablespoons olive oil

Sea salt

1. Preheat the oven to 425°F.
2. Cut the Yukons in half or quarters, depending on their size. You want healthy pieces of potato here. Drop them in a shallow roasting pan, along with the black and green olives, and the olive oil. Give the pan a shake to distribute everything equally. Sprinkle the top with some sea salt.
3. Pop the pan in the oven and roast, shaking the pan once or twice, for 30 minutes, or until the potatoes have browned here and there and they are tender when pierced with a paring knife. These are great hot, but also quite good at room temperature.

TIME: *About 30 minutes*
FEEDS: *4 as a side dish*

Braised Red Peppers

SOMETIMES BELL PEPPERS can be bitter and unpleasant, but a long soak in stock and olive oil gives them a depth and sweetness that surprises. If you're wondering about the anchovies, see the box on page 71.

4 red bell peppers, washed and annoying little stickers peeled off

¼ cup olive oil

½ cup chicken stock

2 cloves garlic, peeled and smashed

1 anchovy fillet packed in olive oil

1. Fire up your stove and put the peppers directly over the flames, charring them, turning them from time to time with a pair of tongs (not your fingers). I use all my burners to get the peppers finished at once. If you have an electric stove, the peppers will blister, not char, but the effect will be the same. When they're sufficiently black all over, drop them in a resealable plastic bag and close the seal, letting them steam for 10 minutes, or until they're cool enough to touch.

2. This is not a dish to make with a fresh manicure. Remove the peppers from the bag, and peel off the charred skin, rinsing off any black bits under a cool tap. Pull off the tops and discard, along with the seeds. Slice the peppers lengthwise into meaty portions.

3. Put the peppers in the bottom of a small saucepan, and cover the slices with the chicken stock, olive oil, garlic cloves, and anchovy fillet. Put the lid on the pot, slightly ajar, and cook the peppers over medium-low heat for 30 minutes. You can reheat them at dinnertime.

TIME: *About an hour, about 15 minutes working time*
FEEDS: *4, as a side dish*

Anchovies

WHAT GIVES THAT sauce it richness? Its depth, its subtle saltiness? That lovely, velvet tang? You might be surprised how often the answer is: an anchovy. Because they melt into nothingness when they're cooked, preserved anchovies are like adding salt, but with a depth of flavor your poor old Morton's couldn't possibly provide. Try the Braised Red Peppers (page 70), and I think you'll agree.

Postcard Placemats

✂

I HAVE A thing for old postcards, which you can collect for pennies at any thrift shop or junk store. The old postmarks, the ancient messages, the mundane images on their fronts (e.g., Grant's Tomb) are somehow charming en masse. This project uses these postal relics, but can be just as easily duplicated with new cards purchased at your local tourist stand or (if you're feeling cultural) art museum.

I should warn you that this project involves field trips to your local stationery store and copy shop (or anywhere else you can get something laminated).

ARTISTIC TALENT METER: MEDIUM

YOU NEED:

48 old, new, or indifferent postcards

Glue stick

File folders (for transportation purposes)

1. For each placemat, you need to arrange nine postcards to form a rectangle: this is the basic placemat, and you should choose the cards you like best, either showing their pictures, or if they're old, the writing on the back, as you see fit. Then, cut and paste the remaining postcards as needed to help close up the seams between the basic postcards. You don't have to be too intense about this, since the whole lot will be laminated.

2. Slide the placemats-to-be into separate folders, and take them to your local copy center, where they can run them through the lamination machine. A little strategic

trimming, and voilà! You have reusable, homemade placemats to enjoy until you get sick of them and want to make new ones.

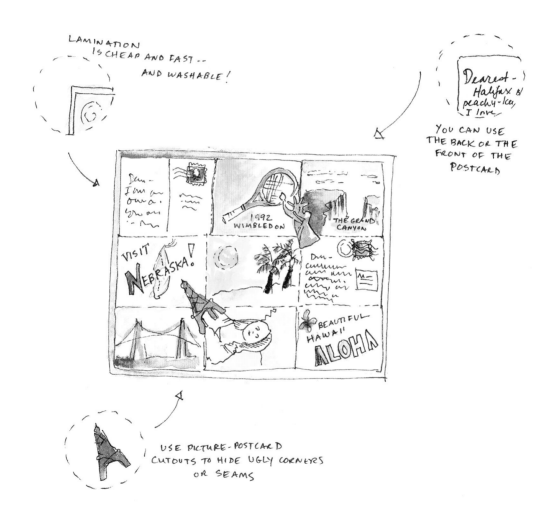

LAMINATION IS CHEAP AND FAST -- AND WASHABLE!

Dearest -
Halifax &
peachy-keen,
I love

YOU CAN USE THE BACK OR THE FRONT OF THE POSTCARD

1992 WIMBLEDON

THE GRAND CANYON

VISIT NEBRASKA!

BEAUTIFUL HAWAII ALOHA

USE PICTURE-POSTCARD CUTOUTS TO HIDE UGLY CORNERS OR SEAMS

Frisée and Baby Greens with Fig Dressing

𝐹IGS SEEM TO pop up with surprising regularity in late fall and early winter in the more chichi grocery stores in my neighborhood. They must be a product of South America, and they sure taste good, a hint of fruity freshness in an otherwise root-and-tuber season. It's worth an extra stroll around your gourmet grocery to see if they're available. If you can't find them, this salad (and particularly the salad dressing) is just as delicious with dried figs substituted for the fresh variety.

1 small head frisée lettuce (chicory), leaves separated, trimmed, washed, and dried

3 cups mixed baby greens

2 shallots, finely minced

2 tablespoons sherry vinegar

8 ripe figs, 4 minced, 4 sliced in half, or 6 dried (see note)

3 tablespoons hazelnut oil

Sea salt and pepper

1. Mix the frisée with the baby greens. Wrap the salad in a kitchen towel and store in the fridge until ready to serve.
2. Several hours before you need the dressing, mix the shallots with sherry vinegar and minced figs in a bowl or small container (I like to use old jam jars here). Right before you serve the salad, finished the salad dressing by drizzling in the hazelnut oil, adding sea salt and pepper to taste, and giving the whole thing a good stir (or shake). Take the wrapped greens out of the fridge and give them a good toss in the dressing. Dot the top of the salad with the halved figs, and serve with some good bread and cheese.

TIME: *A few hours, almost entirely unattended; about 10 minutes of actual preparation time*

FEEDS: *4*

NOTE: *Dried figs are delicious but stronger in flavor than fresh, so if you are using dried figs, use only two minced, macerated in the same way as the fresh. You can plump up the dried figs for the top of the salad in a bath of hot water and a drizzle of honey.*

THE TWO OF US . . . AND FRIENDS

Brown Sugar Pudding with Raspberries

*P*UDDING IS A crowd-pleaser. This one is very rich, so you only need dole out a dollop. Top the pudding generously with the raspberries.

3 cups whole milk

1 vanilla bean, split lengthwise

6 egg yolks

⅓ cup granulated sugar

½ cup light brown sugar

¼ teaspoon salt

¼ cup cornstarch

1 tablespoon cold unsalted butter

A pint of raspberries, picked over and washed

1. Pour the milk into a medium-size saucepan, add the split vanilla bean, and bring the milk to a boil. Watch it like a hawk so that half the milk doesn't end up scalded to your cooktop. As soon as it boils, turn off the heat and cover the pan tightly. Let it sit for 15 minutes, allowing the vanilla to steep in the milk.

2. Meanwhile, in a mixing bowl, beat the egg yolks until lemon-colored and satiny, either with a whisk or an electric mixer. Add the sugars, and beat until combined. Add the salt and cornstarch, mixing until no streaks or lumps of cornstarch remain.

3. Pour a ladleful of the hot milk into the eggs, whisking energetically all the while. Add the rest of the milk, then pour the custard back into the pot through a fine-mesh sieve to catch any lumps and bumps. Bring the pudding to a boil over medium heat and stir continuously, paying extra-special attention to the corners of the pot. Cook until the cornstarch kicks in and the pudding starts to thicken, about 3 minutes. Remove from the heat and stir in the cold butter.

4. Pour the pudding into a small bowl, and cover with plastic wrap—make sure the plastic touches the top of the pudding or else you'll have a skin. Refrigerate for at least 3 hours before eating.

5. Right before serving, mash the raspberries lightly with the back of a fork. Dish up a heaping serving-spoonful of pudding, and top with several squished raspberries.

TIME: *4 hours, mostly refridgeration time*
FEEDS: *4*

Spring Forward

Lemon-Ricotta Ravioli with Green Beans and Mozzarella (page 77)
Duck Legs Braised in White Wine (page 82)
Caramelized Fennel (page 85)
Roasted Strawberries with Balsamic Vinegar and Brown Sugar (page 86)

Like flowers, love is in bloom in spring, and you better look out, because you never know what will happen when strangers meet at your dinner table. We introduced two friends, Mike and Dune, at our dinner table one spring, and two years later they got married. Though JS takes all credit for this felicitous pairing, I'm now happily retired as a matchmaker, with a 100 percent success rate.

Another time, we had my friend Jordan and her boyfriend, Pierre, to dinner. As I knew Pierre very little, I sat him next to me so I could size up whether I approved of him for my friend. My clever scheme soon backfired: he was silent as the grave, six feet four inches of stone. He barely cracked a smile all night, sending me into hostess panic: Did he hate me? Or worse, did he hate my food?

The mystery of Pierre was solved twenty-four hours later: Jordan called, now an engaged lady. Obviously, Pierre had been understandably preoccupied with the upcoming proposal the night before. We have since had many lovely conversations at my dinner table, and I even conned him into hosting a party at their apartment, since ours is the size of a postage stamp (more about that party on page 216). So if you want anybody to get married, or you, yourself, are thinking about getting married, have a springtime dinner party. I can vouch for the results.

Lemon-Ricotta Ravioli with Green Beans and Mozzarella

𝒯HIS IS A two-part dish: First, you make some quick homemade ravioli using frozen wonton skins—three per person—then you assemble a little salad of young greens, peas, and haricots verts. Finally, you add a very light dressing and some very fresh mozzarella, the kind that comes packaged in water.

FOR THE RAVIOLI:

1 cup whole-milk ricotta cheese

Zest of 1 lemon

¼ teaspoon freshly grated nutmeg

½ teaspoon kosher salt

½ cup freshly grated Parmesan cheese

¼ cup chopped fresh parsley

1 egg

1 package of small wonton skins

FOR THE SALAD:

1 teaspoon kosher salt

1 cup sugar snap peas, trimmed

12 ounces haricots verts or other green beans, trimmed

1 cup freshly shelled peas, or "fancy" frozen ones

2 small heads Bibb lettuce, outer leaves removed and discarded, the rest washed and dried

12 ounces very fresh mozzarella (from the deli counter, not the dairy case), sliced

FOR THE DRESSING:

¼ cup highest-quality olive oil

A squeeze of lemon

1 tablespoon chopped fresh tarragon

½ teaspoon chopped fresh oregano

1 tablespoon chopped fresh parsley

Sea salt and pepper

1. Make the filling for the ravioli: combine the ricotta, lemon zest, nutmeg, salt, Parmesan, and parsley in a small bowl, then taste and correct for salt. Mix in the egg.
2. Fill a little bowl with cold tap water and open the package of wonton skins. Line up several in a row, then put a heaping teaspoonful of filling on the middle of each one. Dip your index finger in the water, moisten the edges of each wonton skin, then fold it over on itself and press down to seal the ravioli. Continue with the remaining filling and skins. Your aim is three per person, plus a couple of

extra, in case of emergency or seconds. Let your ravioli rest on a cookie rack at room temperature until you need them.

3. Prep the salad: Fill a large bowl with ice water, then bring a skillet full of water to a boil, add the kosher salt, and blanch the following in this order: the sugar snap peas, for 2 minutes; the haricots verts, for 1½ minutes, and the peas for 30 seconds. Drain them all and toss them in the ice water to stop the cooking.

4. Make the dressing: Mix the olive oil, lemon juice, chopped herbs, and salt and pepper to taste in a small bowl and set aside.

5. Right before you're going to eat, bring a large pot of water to a boil, adding a tablespoon of oil, along with a handful of kosher salt. Throw in the ravioli and set your egg timer for 3 minutes. On a platter or in a shallow bowl, arrange the lettuce leaves, curved side up, so they act like little bowls. Artfully strew the peas and beans over the top. Lay the sliced mozzarella in the middle of this salad, and, when the buzzer goes off, drain the ravioli and add them to the mix. Drizzle on the dressing, then toss very lightly, making sure not to destroy your beautiful ravioli in the process. Everybody should get three ravioli, one slice of mozz, and a healthy helping of beans, peas, and lettuce.

TIME: *An hour of puttering around the kitchen, but everything's make-ahead except for dressing and assembling the salad and boiling the ravioli*
FEEDS: *6 as a first course*

Pasta Salads with Attitude

*R*ule one of cool pasta salads: no shredded carrots. Rule two: no Miracle Whip. Here are three elegant pasta salad suggestions to get you thinking about the world beyond the school cafeteria:

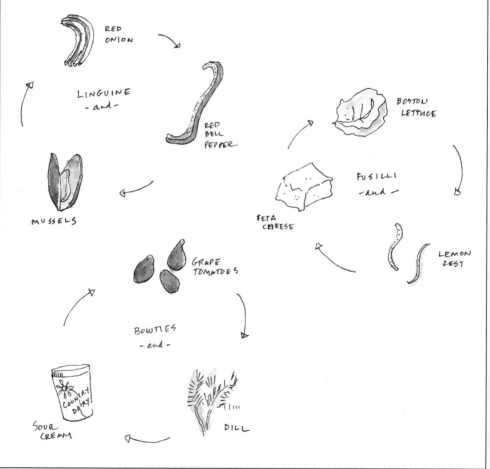

RED ONION

LINGUINE
- and -

RED BELL PEPPER

BOSTON LETTUCE

FUSILLI
- and -

FETA CHEESE

MUSSELS

LEMON ZEST

GRAPE TOMATOES

BOWTIES
- and -

SOUR CREAM

COUNTRY DAIRY

DILL

Lemon Votives

THESE LITTLE ONE-OFF votives are charming, and delicately perfume the air with lemon as the natural oils in the lemon rind heat up. This takes a bit of dexterity, but even lopsided lemon votives are cute and prove that you made them yourself.

ARTISTIC TALENT METER: MEDIUM

YOU NEED:

3 nice, big unblemished lemons

A paring knife

A teaspoon

A vegetable peeler

A 2-inch biscuit cutter (optional)

Unscented tea lights, in their little tin containers

1. Lay the lemons on their sides like little boats and decide which end is up: usually, there's a flatter angle which, helped along, can be used as the bottom of the votive. Once you're satisfied, cut the top third off each lemon.

2. Take the knife and carefully begin to pry the fruit away from the pith and rind. It's important to do this with some patience, because you can't let the lemon rip. It can be helpful to use the spoon, particularly in the bottom part (the future candle holder). When all the lemon flesh is scooped out, clean up the edges with your vegetable peeler. All in all, this little operation should take you about 5 minutes per lemon.

3. Set the now-emptied lemon down on the counter. If it really rocks and rolls, trim a little patch of rind off the bottom to give it a base. Take the cap and, using your knife or the 2-inch biscuit cutter, cut a vent in the lemon peel, so when you light the candle you don't have flaming lemons on your table. If you cut it out with a knife, make sure to be generous. If I'm free-forming it, I like to cut the hole into a pointed oval, a sort of artist's rendition of what a lemon's shape is. Of course, if you have little cookie cutters in the shape of stars or hearts, you could use those here.

4. Let the lemons dry for a few hours on your counter. When you're ready to use them, set the tea lights inside, light them, and replace the lemon caps. The lemons should glow prettily, and the vent in the top should be large enough to avoid singeing. They'll last you as long as the tea light is burning.

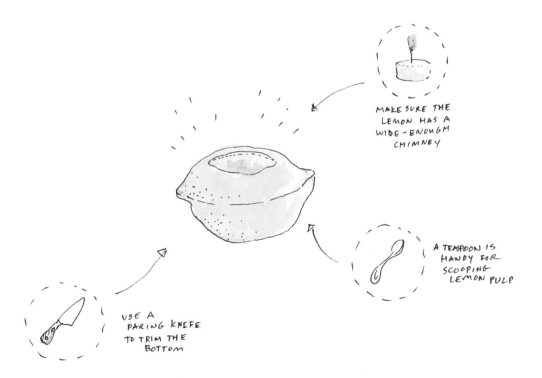

MAKE SURE THE LEMON HAS A WIDE-ENOUGH CHIMNEY

A TEASPOON IS HANDY FOR SCOOPING LEMON PULP

USE A PARING KNIFE TO TRIM THE BOTTOM

Duck Legs Braised in White Wine

As you can see, this recipe doesn't call for many ingredients. The trick is the way you treat the duck, which takes a little patience but is amply rewarding. Duck legs are quite big and meaty, and fill a good niche, tastewise, between chicken and beef. Besides, it's fun to surprise friends with something out of the ordinary. You can usually buy duck legs in vacuum packs, and they will freeze very well.

4 duck legs, trimmed of extra fat

1 clove garlic, crushed

Several sprigs fresh thyme

1 teaspoon kosher salt

Pepper

½ cup white wine

1. Heat a large skillet over high heat while you prep the duck: prick the skin all over the legs, going only as deep as the fat layer under the skin. Go ahead, go crazy—treat those legs as impromptu voodoo dolls. Lay them in the hot pan, skin side down, turn down the heat to medium, and sear them, without disturbing, for 15 minutes. You'll be shocked to see the lake of duck fat that is rendered. For this, you should make sure you have an old milk carton or other nonmeltable, disposable container on hand. Take the duck legs out of the pan, set them aside on a platter, and drain all of the fat out of the pan into your receptacle. Wipe out the pan using a piece of paper towel held with tongs.
2. Return the pan to the fire and add the garlic. After 30 seconds, return the duck legs to the pan, this time skin side up, and add the thyme, salt, several grindings of fresh pepper, and white wine. Reduce the heat to a minimum, put a lid on the skillet, leaving it slightly ajar, and cook for an hour.
3. At the end of the hour, lift the legs out of the braising liquid and degrease the sauce by tilting the pan and spooning off the fat with a soup spoon. Be diligent about this, taking a few minutes to really get as much duck fat as you can. Taste the sauce and correct for salt. Pour the sauce into a small pot and let it sit on a back burner at low heat.

4. Right before serving, reheat the duck legs over medium heat, skin side down, in the original skillet, to crisp up the skin a bit. Serve with a spoonful or two of the reserved sauce over the top.

TIME: *More than an hour, much of it unattended*
FEEDS: *4*

Flower Power:
TULIPS

IN THE MOVIE version of *A Room with a View*, the romance novelist Eleanor Lavish (played by Judi Dench), when asked what flowers she prefers, proclaims, "The reckless rose! The tempestuous tulip!"

I love that line because, is there any flower less tempestuous? How many times have you shoved a bouquet of corner-store tulips into a glass pitcher, and called it a day? The problem with tulips is that they're burdened with too many long leaves, making the lovely flower heads an afterthought. So strip them away! Buy two bunches rather than one, and snip away the leaves with kitchen scissors, letting the tulips spill over the side of a pitcher all in one direction. Without all that greenery, the tulips open more quickly, and, spilling dramatically over the side of a pitcher, these corner-store pickups do become, well, tempestuous.

Most Wanted
The Over-Stayer
AKA MR. 2:00 AM, THE LAST MAN STANDING

Subject is easily recognized by the fact that he or she is the last person remaining in host's house, even though all candles are gutted, the music has been turned off, and hostess is either in her nightgown or actually asleep. Subject can aggravate situation by ignoring the host's washing a large pile of dishes in sink, and by repeating a lengthy story already told before the main course. How to tame the Over-Stayer? Host can gently hint of need to rise early the next morning, then ask if subject could lend a helping hand to tidy up the kitchen. This sweetly phrased threat usually convinces even the tardiest sort to leave.

Caramelized Fennel

RAW FENNEL, SHAVED into salads, has a zip to it, a definite anise taste that's very bright on the palate. Cooked, however, it's sweet and mellow, and a perfect accompaniment to the rich, almost beefy flavor of the duck legs.

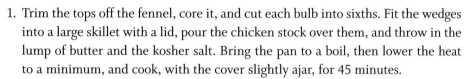

4 small bulbs fennel, stalk fronds reserved and chopped

½ cup chicken stock

2 tablespoons unsalted butter

½ teaspoon kosher salt

1. Trim the tops off the fennel, core it, and cut each bulb into sixths. Fit the wedges into a large skillet with a lid, pour the chicken stock over them, and throw in the lump of butter and the kosher salt. Bring the pan to a boil, then lower the heat to a minimum, and cook, with the cover slightly ajar, for 45 minutes.
2. At the end of 45 minutes, check the pan. The stock should have boiled away and left a shiny glaze on the fennel. Toss with a handful of the reserved fennel fronds and dish it up. You can make this ahead and reheat right before serving.

TIME: *About 45 minutes, mostly unattended*

FEEDS: *4 as a side dish*

SWEET AND SOUR COMBINATIONS

LOTS OF FRUITS benefit from some sourness—it gives them depth of flavor, providing an unexpected counterpoint to their unadulterated sweetness. It's not unlike Paul McCartney and John Lennon. With John, Paul was the Walrus. Without him? Wings. Here are two fruit and acid combinations worth giving a try:

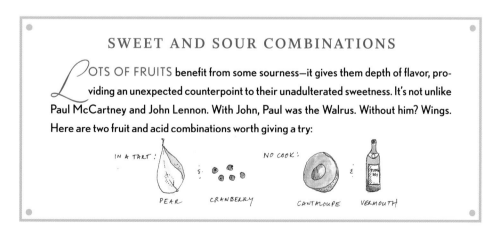

IN A TART: PEAR   CRANBERRY   NO COOK: CANTALOUPE   VERMOUTH

Roasted Strawberries with Balsamic Vinegar and Brown Sugar

$\mathcal{E}$VEN IN SEASON, the mass-market strawberries available, while looking impressively red and robust, can taste more like paper pulp than a self-respecting spring fruit. But all is not lost: adding some balsamic vinegar and brown sugar returns some dignity to these strawberries, intensifying both their tartness and sweetness.

2 pints large strawberries, hulled
¼ cup balsamic vinegar

6 tablespoons dark brown sugar
1 tablespoon butter

1. Preheat the oven to 450°F.
2. Hull the strawberries, and line them up, pointy ends up, in a small baking dish. The more crowded the strawberries are, the better.
3. Drizzle the balsamic over the tops of the strawberries, then sprinkle brown sugar around, making sure to press some down in the canyons between the strawberries. Dot the top with butter.
4. Roast the strawberries, checking them from time to time for softness, for about 20 minutes. You want them to have given up their juice, but the integrity of the berry should be intact. When you serve them, make sure to spoon up the wonderful sweet-tart strawberry syrup in the bottom of the baking dish and pour it over the berries.

TIME: *About 30 minutes*
FEEDS: *4*

Peaks of Summer

Gazpacho with Almonds (page 88)

TROUT, THREE WAYS:
Baked Trout with Herbs (page 90)

or

Fried Trout with Sizzled Sage (page 93)

or

Trout Poached with Cream and Cucumber (page 94)

Easy Green Bean Salad (page 96)
White Peach Brûlée (page 100)

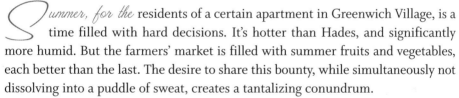

Summer, for the residents of a certain apartment in Greenwich Village, is a time filled with hard decisions. It's hotter than Hades, and significantly more humid. But the farmers' market is filled with summer fruits and vegetables, each better than the last. The desire to share this bounty, while simultaneously not dissolving into a puddle of sweat, creates a tantalizing conundrum.

Here's the bottom line: If people come over to the apartment in August, they better be wearing a tank top and little else. Our valiant little air conditioner does its best, but, to be truthful, it can do nothing when confronted by the raging furnace that is my extremely small four-burner gas stove. The summertime solution? Try, at all costs, to avoid turning on the stove when people are over. And if it does have to go on, make it a five-minutes-or-less scenario. And to ease your friends' discomfort, make sure to ply them with extra white wine, kept as cold as possible. Because it would be a shame to keep these treats of summer all to yourself.

Gazpacho with Almonds

𝒢ROWING UP, WE had gazpacho occasionally, mostly a sort of extra-pureed salsa that sat, lumpy and thick, in the bowl. It was only later, in Spain, that I tasted really good gazpacho, meaning not a recipe that came with the Osterizer blender in 1971. Real gazpacho is thinner than those Americanized versions, and can be thickened with old bread, soaked and pureed, or ground almonds, which I prefer because it adds sweetness as well as body.

SOUP:

⅔ cup blanched slivered almonds

2½ pounds summer beefsteak tomatoes, extremely ripe

4 cloves garlic

⅓ cup extra-virgin olive oil

1 medium-size cucumber, peeled and diced

1 tablespoon sherry vinegar

Sea salt and pepper

TOPPING:

1 yellow bell pepper

1. Pulverize the blanched almonds in your food processor, really blitzing them until there are no large pieces left. Measure out ½ cup and set aside.
2. Peel and seed the tomatoes: drop the tomatoes in boiling water for 30 seconds, and their skins will come right off. Cut the tomatoes in half and squeeze them gently. Use your fingers to get rid of most of the seeds. Cut the tomatoes into a large dice, and put them in a saucepan, along with three of the garlic cloves and the olive oil. Cook over low heat for 10 minutes, until the tomatoes just begin to release their juice.
3. Pour the tomatoes into the food processor bowl, and add the cucumber, sherry, and salt and pepper to taste. Give everything a whiz, then grate the remaining garlic clove into the bowl and blitz again. Finally, add ⅓ cup of water and the ground almonds, and pour into a bowl, cover, and chill in the fridge for at least 2 hours.
4. Hold the bell pepper over an open flame and char it all over, turning it with tongs, not your delicate fingers. When it is sufficiently blackened, seal it in an old paper bag or resealable plastic bag until it cools, about 10 minutes. Then peel it, trying not to rinse it too much, seed it, and cut it into long, thin tendrils. When you serve the soup, top it with a few curls of this roasted pepper.

TIME: *20 minutes working time, several hours chilling-out time*
FEEDS: *Makes 4 hearty portions*

GAZPACHO ADD-INS

J'VE BEEN STINGY in the above recipe, including only one topping. When I was a kid, the toppings were where it was at. Consider broadening your horizons and including some others:

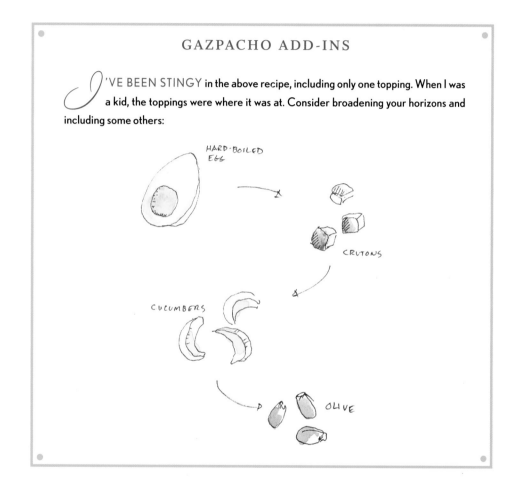

nstead of just one main course with this menu, I wanted to show you a riff on one summer ingredient. Brook trout is a perfect summertime ingredient: not only is the flesh light and delicate, but it's available at farmers' markets, just pulled out of the water.

Trout lends itself to several different cooking techniques, but the main thing to keep in mind is not to overcook it. It's tastiest when it has just a hint of other flavor to round it out, and when it's accompanied by the simplest side dishes.

Trout #1

Baked Trout with Herbs

SOMETIMES, I DO a whole rigmarole with a salt crust, but I think this bed of salt and herbs works just as well. Unlike a bigger fish—a whole snapper, for instance—the trout is in the oven so briefly that it won't dry out, one of the principal reasons for encasing fish in salt. Baking it on a bed of salt, however, helps the herbs to perfume the fish.

This dish is very open to improvisation—in the summer it's easy to be very flexible about which herbs you use.

6 cups coarse kosher salt

4 small whole brook trout (about 1 pound each)

Several bunches of a few of the following: chives, parsley, chervil, oregano, dill, mint, tarragon, sage

Sea salt and pepper

Lemon wedges, for serving

1/4 pound (1 stick) unsalted butter, for the sauce

1. Preheat the oven to 425°F. Prepare a roasting pan big enough to hold all the fish by pouring the coarse kosher into it and swishing it around into an even layer.

2. Wash the trout, inside and out, and pat dry. Salt and pepper the cavities, then stuff the cavities full of an herb bouquet of your choice—the only usual suspects I've omitted are rosemary and cilantro, because they are so strong they'll over-power the fish. Tuck the herbs in firmly, then secure the fish with a toothpick. Place the whole fish side by side on the salt.
3. Into the oven go the trout, where they should roast for 25 minutes, until they're firm when you press down on the side with a finger.
4. While they're cooking, make a bit of brown butter: melt the stick of butter in a small saucepan over medium-low heat. The butter will melt, separate, and then the solids will start to brown. When the solids are nut brown and the clarified butter is lightly sherry-colored, it's ready, 8 to 10 minutes.
5. Give everyone a whole trout, lifting it off the salt bed using two spatulas at once, and then consult my scientific diagram on how to deal with a whole fish (see page 92). Serve with lemon wedges and the brown butter on the side.

TIME: *About 30 minutes*
FEEDS: *4, amply*

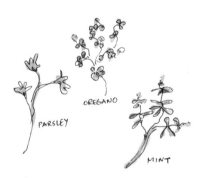

FILLETING A TROUT

You, too, can fillet with the panache of a French restaurateur: First, turn the fish so that it is parallel to you on the plate. Making delicate cuts, separate the head from the body, cut down the length of the spine, and then slice through the tail. Using your knife and fork as makeshift tongs, carefully lever the top fillet off the bottom one, working it loose from the spine and flipping it over so it lies skin side down on the plate. Pull up the head, which has the added bonus of taking the spine and tail with it, and return that debris to the platter. Take a few minutes and cut away any fine bones that might be lurking near the edges of the trout fillet, squeeze a bit of lemon and add a few grains of coarse sea salt, and you've got yourself a filleted fish.

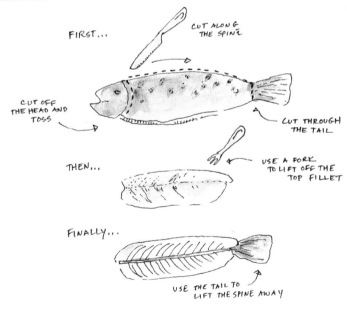

FIRST...

CUT ALONG THE SPINE

CUT OFF THE HEAD AND TOSS

CUT THROUGH THE TAIL

THEN...

USE A FORK TO LIFT OFF THE TOP FILLET

FINALLY...

USE THE TAIL TO LIFT THE SPINE AWAY

Trout #2
Fried Trout with Sizzled Sage

*T*HE SOUTHERN STANDARD for coating fried trout is cornmeal, but the more refined, softer semolina is an elegant substitution for a dinner party.

4 trout fillets	**1 tablespoon butter**
¼ cup milk	**20 fresh sage leaves**
1 cup semolina flour	**Salt and pepper**
1 tablespoon vegetable oil	

1. Pour the milk into a shallow dish, and the semolina flour onto a dinner plate. Salt and pepper the trout fillets well, dip them first in the milk, then coat them well in the semolina. Set aside for a moment.
2. In a large nonstick skillet—you might have to fry the trout in batches—melt the butter in the vegetable oil over medium-high heat. When the foaming has subsided, slip in the prepared trout fillets. Fry them until golden, about 4 minutes per side. In the last 2 minutes of cooking, slip the sage leaves into the hot fat, and watch them sizzle.
3. To serve, top the prettily browned fillets with a pinch of sea salt and several sizzled sage leaves.

TIME: *About 10 minutes*
FEEDS: *4*

Trout #3

Trout Poached with Cream and Cucumber

*T*HIS IS THE most delicate of the trout dishes, because the poaching works with the natural softness of the trout.

4 trout fillets

1 bay leaf

½ teaspoon whole peppercorns, crushed

1 teaspoon kosher salt

1 cup heavy cream

½ cup dry white wine

A large hothouse cucumber, split in half lengthwise, seeded, and cut into crescents

¼ cup coarsely chopped fresh mint

1. Nestle the trout fillets side by side in a lidded skillet large enough to fit them all. Add the bay leaf, peppercorns, kosher salt, heavy cream, and white wine, and bring to a lazy boil over medium-low heat. Cook, uncovered, for 8 minutes.
2. At that point, add the cucumbers, tucking them gently here and there among the fillets. Cover the pan and cook for 5 minutes more.
3. To serve, carefully lift the fillets out of the pan using a long spatula. Spoon some cream sauce on top, including a good portion of cucumbers. Sprinkle on some sea salt and chopped mint. Eat right away.

TIME: *About 15 minutes*

FEEDS: *4*

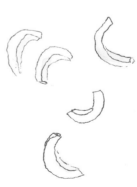

Summer Vegetable Cheat Sheet

Forthwith, a list of summer vegetables, and how best to eat them:

TOMATOES: Sprinkle with coarse sea salt and the merest touch of olive oil.

CORN: Plunge into boiling water for no more than three minutes, day of purchase. Butter, pepper, salt.

CUCUMBERS: Peel, seed, slice, and toss lightly with white wine vinegar and sea salt.

ZUCCHINI: Slice, salt, let sit for 15 minutes, then brush with olive oil and grill in a hot pan, a minute on each side.

EGGPLANT: Cube, salt the cubes, and let drain for 30 minutes, rinse, then quickly sauté in olive oil and add a bit of salt and parsley.

SPINACH: Wash but don't dry it, and throw it in a hot skillet for 1 minute. Serve with sea salt and a lemon wedge.

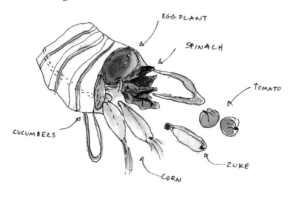

Easy Green Bean Salad

*T*HERE ARE PILES and piles of green beans at any self-respecting farm stand in the height of summer. So fresh that they need very little cooking, these beans only ask for a quick steam and then a bath in salad dressing while they're still warm. Serve them at room temperature, either as a side dish or as a salad course.

1½ pounds green beans, trimmed

1 clove garlic

1 tablespoon balsamic vinegar

1 tablespoon hazelnut or extra-virgin olive oil

Sea salt

1. Set up your steamer—either the metal kind that goes inside the pot, or the cheaply purchased Asian bamboo steamer—and bring a few inches of water to a boil. Add the prepped green beans and close the lid. Cook for 3 minutes.

2. Meanwhile grate the garlic clove into a dish that can subsequently hold the beans, then add the vinegar and the oil. Add a pinch of sea salt. When the beans have steamed for 3 minutes, toss them immediately into the bowl and coat well with the dressing. Taste for salt. Serve warm or at room temperature.

TIME: *About 15 minutes of working time*
FEEDS: *4, as a side dish or salad*

Mosquitoes and You, Perfect Together

*I*F YOU EAT outside in the summer, you know the drill. It's a beautiful evening, the light taking its time to completely dissolve from the sky, and you're sitting on somebody's porch enjoying listening to the ice cubes clink together in your gin and tonic. And then . . . a sharp pain shoots up your ankle, or you feel a persistent nibbling at your toes. Mosquitoes. Those citronella candles or little incense rings are all well and good, but if you want to be a truly considerate host, have a bottle of Avon's Skin So Soft within easy reach and offer the lotion around the table before the little vampires come in for the kill. It'll make that summer dinner that much better.

Fruit Centerpieces

IN THE SUMMER, the flowers are cheap but the fruit is cheaper. The most important thing for these centerpieces—more important than the fruit, almost—is that it comes in cute paper or wooden boxes. If you happen upon some at a farmers' market, save them for when all you can find are ugly plastic boxes.

ARTISTIC TALENT METER: LOW

YOU NEED:

2 pint baskets, and 1 quart basket of small summer fruit: plums, apricots, grapes, figs, large berries
1 egg white
½ cup sugar
Several yards of pretty grosgrain ribbon
Several sheets of paper towels
Scissors

1. All you need to do here is make the fruit look like the best darn fruit there ever was. Empty the baskets carefully, washing and picking through the fruit. Set five perfect specimens aside for a moment.

2. Crumple up some paper towels and place them in the bottom of your baskets. This will give the fruit a little more height and provide a nice mounding effect in the baskets. Fill the cartons back up with the fruit, save the reserved beauties, and tie a bow around the middle of each carton—I like to do a pretty knot, rather than a full-fledged Christmas-present bow. The boxes should be arranged on the table with the larger one between the two smaller ones.

3. Take the egg white and whisk it with 2 teaspoons of water in a shallow bowl. Pour the sugar onto a dinner plate, and set up a cookie rack on your counter. Make sure that the remaining five fruits are perfectly dry, then roll the fruit, one by one, entirely in the egg white, then in the sugar. Let the sugared fruits dry completely on the cookie rack, then add them to your cartons: three for the large one, and one each for the smaller ones.

4. The reaction to this centerpiece is well out of proportion for the amount of time and effort expended, believe me.

USE A COOKIE RACK TO DRY THE SUGARED FRUIT

YOU CAN WASH OFF THE SUGAR AND EAT THE FRUIT THE NEXT DAY

YOU CAN SAVE WOODEN BASKETS AND RE-USE THEM

A KNOT IS LESS FUSSY THAN A BOW

White Peach Brûlée

$\mathcal{G}$IVING SUMMER-RIPE peaches a little goose with some brown sugar and butter makes an already wonderful fruit perfect.

4 white peaches, ripe as you can find

8 teaspoons butter

1 cup brown sugar

½ cup heavy cream or crème fraîche

1. If you're using a conventional oven, preheat the broiler. If you're using a toaster oven, plug it in.
2. Bring a pot of water to a boil. Make a little X at the base of each peach (this makes them easier to peel), then drop them in the boiling water. Let them bob there for a minute, then rescue them with a slotted spoon and run them under cold water. Peel them, cut them in half, and arrange them on a baking sheet, or on the baking pan in your toaster oven (my endless adulations for the toaster oven continue here).
3. Dot the top of each peach with a teaspoon of butter and a tablespoon of brown sugar. Slide under the broiler or toaster oven broiler for 5 minutes, until the sugar is bubbling and has darkened. Serve the peaches in soup bowls with a drizzle of heavy cream or a dollop of crème fraîche.

TIME: *About 10 minutes*

FEEDS: *4*

Fall Lunch Hours

Chestnut Soup with Crème Fraîche and Fennel Seeds (page 102)
Pan-Roasted Whole Chicken Legs (page 104)
Sautéed Savoy Cabbage (page 108)
Salt-Roasted Root Vegetables (page 109)
Radicchio Salad (page 111)
Chocolatey Floating Island (page 112)

Our friend Dune is an impressive napper. As the clock creeps toward midnight, particularly if I've given her the comfy chair (we have only one), I'll look up from my one-too-many glasses of red wine and see her peacefully dozing, in the middle of the dinner-party din. She sleeps through broken china. She sleeps through warbling renditions of "Jesus Christ, Superstar" by her husband and mine. She even sleeps through the inevitable playing of the immortal hair-band classic, Mr. Big's "(I'm the One Who Wants to) Be with You" at top volume, the traditional sign-off of another good dinner party.

Dune's problem is that, unlike the other ne'er-do-wells around the table, she is impressively employed and must get to the office at 5:30 AM. So it's a lot to ask that she stay awake until it's time to leave. But her need for shut-eye made me scheme to find a way to see Dune awake through the entirety of a meal. Then I thought of a creative solution: lunch!

So this menu was created to get you nice and full at a long, lazy lunch, with no worries of waking up in six hours to play tennis or pick up the dry cleaning or (God forbid) go to the office. There's plenty of extra that can be sent home with your friends, so they can pick out of the fridge at ten at night and be perfectly content.

The dinner-party lunch. I'm going to start a revolution.

Chestnut Soup with Crème Fraîche and Fennel Seeds

 $\mathcal{I}$ 'M A CHESTNUT obsessive. There's just something about them—their creaminess, their delicate sweetness—that makes me very, very happy. When you cook with them, and decide not to roast them yourself, try to find peeled chestnuts that have been vacuum packed into jars or foil packets, not in cans, because the canned chestnuts take a major hit in terms of texture.

2 tablespoons butter

2 shallots, chopped

½ head fennel, trimmed, cored, and finely chopped

1 teaspoon salt

1 tablespoon all-purpose flour

1 sprig thyme

1 tablespoon fennel seeds

6 cups good-quality chicken stock

2 (8-ounce) jars vacuum-packed chestnuts, 6 chestnuts rescued from one jar and set aside

6 tablespoons crème fraîche or sour cream

A handful of parsley, chopped

1. In a large saucepan that can subsequently hold all the stock, sauté the shallots and fennel in 1 tablespoon of the butter and the kosher salt for 5 minutes over medium-high heat, until the vegetables are truly translucent. Sprinkle the flour over the top, then stir to coat the veggies and to cook off the taste of the flour.

2. Crush the chestnuts with the back of a fork, then toss them into the pot, along with the thyme, and 1 tablespoon of the fennel seeds. Give them a turn in the sautéed vegetables. Then slowly pour in the chicken stock, bring the pot to a simmer, and allow the soup to cook for 30 minutes.

3. In batches, ladle the soup into a food processor or blender, pureeing until the soup is generally smooth—a few little chunks here or there is perfectly acceptable. Pour the soup back into the pot and keep warm until you need it.

4. Melt the remaining tablespoon of butter in a small pan and, when the foam has subsided, slip in the reserved chestnuts. Give them a good sauté, about 5 minutes, until they turn a shiny brown. To serve the soup, ladle it into bowls, add a

tablespoon of crème fraîche in the middle, add a sautéed chestnut, and sprinkle the top with a bit of chopped parsley.

~

TIME: *45 minutes or less*
FEEDS: *6*
SPECIAL EQUIPMENT: *A blender or food processor. One of those immersion blenders would save washing a dirty bowl here, too.*

Flower Power
DAHLIAS

DAHLIAS START POPPING up in late August and continue through the late fall. They are saturated in color and make a very striking bouquet, particularly if you can get your hands on several blooms in the same color family. When you get them home, clean the stems quite thoroughly, because dahlias have a tendency to get slimy. Mass them tightly, and make sure to choose a vase where they'll fit snugly. Add a teaspoon of bleach and a tablespoon of sugar to the water, then arrange the trimmed dahlias. Finally, make sure to change the water every day.

=DAHLIA=

Pan-Roasted Whole Chicken Legs

*B*Y "WHOLE" I mean "whole": chicken legs and thighs that have not been separated. This dish has two virtues: first, it's cheap as can be, and second, it's easy as pie. Actually, easier, as anyone who makes short crust can tell you.

4 whole chicken legs, including thighs, skin on	2 tablespoons olive oil
4 cloves garlic, 2 minced, 2 lightly crushed	1 tablespoon unsalted butter
1½ teaspoons kosher salt	2 sprigs rosemary
Pepper	¼ cup dry white wine

1. Wash and dry the chicken legs, patting them all over very carfully with paper towel. Then, using your fingers, loosen the skin over the thigh and drumstick carefully, making sure not to tear it. Take a fingerful of the minced garlic, and rub it under the skin. Salt and pepper the chicken liberally.

2. Heat the olive oil and butter in a large, deep-sided, lidded skillet until the butter's foam subsides. Then slip in the chicken, in batches if necessary. The heat here should be turned up and down as the pan tells you it needs to be turned—scary, aggressive spitting suggests a lower flame, while sluggish bubbling needs a bit of fire. Be careful and try not to scorch the skin, but give the legs a good, deep browning on both sides.

3. Reduce the heat to low. Arrange the browned legs skin side up in the pan. Give the rosemary sprigs a good crush and twist in your fist, and tuck them among the chicken legs; add the 2 crushed garlic cloves and the small bit of white wine. Cover the pan and cook, checking once or twice, for 30 minutes.

4. At this point, leave the lid ajar, and cook for another 10 minutes, shaking the pan to ensure the legs aren't sticking. The wine should have disappeared, but if the pan is bone dry, add a drop of water to prevent any burning (particularly of the garlic). You can check the doneness by wiggling a drumstick (it should shimmy easily) or, more scientifically, using your trusty meat thermometer—175°F is right on the money.

5. Transfer the legs to a serving plate, pick the rosemary sprigs out of the pan, and pour in ½ cup of water. Cook over medium-high heat, scraping up the goodies on the bottom of the pan and crushing the cooked garlic cloves with the back of a wooden spoon to make a nice gravy. Serve over the chicken legs.

~

TIME: *About an hour*
FEEDS: *4*
SPECIAL EQUIPMENT: *Not so keen on scrubbing spattered chicken fat off your backsplash? Invest in a spatter screen, a piece of wire mesh on a skillet-size loop that will keep the fat where it should be, in the pan.*

Easy Table Runners

IF YOU HAVE a nice tabletop, this easy runner is a good alternative to placemats, or the whole to-do of getting out and pressing a tablecloth. I used old cloth cocktail or luncheon napkins to make this runner, which are widely available for very little money at local junk and vintage stores, and at your local flea market. They are often embroidered with jokey little motifs—olives, cocktail shakers—that are very 1950s, the last era when people used cloth cocktail napkins. In the summer, you might think to do this with vintage hankies—so many have never been used, and the light white squares look pretty marching down a table.

One more thing: I call for buttons here; if you need a source, try mandjtrimmings.com, an astounding store and Web site devoted to sewing notions. But you can always use the old buttons in your sewing kit that belong to shirts and pants long tossed away.

ARTISTIC TALENT METER: MEDIUM

YOU'LL NEED:

Cocktail napkins, about 10 inches square when unfolded (you can mix and match vintage finds, in a patchwork)

An ironing board and iron, with plenty of steam

Straight pins

Needle and thread

Scissors

Fabric glue

An assortment of buttons

1. The width and length of your runner is more easily decided by the size of your table than by me. To figure out what you need, measure the length of your table, and add 24 inches —you want the runner to hang 12 inches off each end of your table. As to width, ideally the runner should be a third as wide as the table, so chances are, you'll need two napkins across. Count on needing at least a dozen napkins.

2. Iron the napkins very flat, using lots of steam from your iron. Lay them out on your table, and decide on your pattern. Pin the napkins together at the inside corners, where four napkins come together, but leave the outside corners unpinned.

3. Take your needle and thread and sew these points together. You don't need great sewing technique here, as this is not the Bayeux tapestry and your pitiful stitching will be covered by the button anyway. Dot these junctions with a small squeeze of fabric glue, and press a button down on top. Once the glue has dried (check your brand for specific timing) you are ready to run the table.

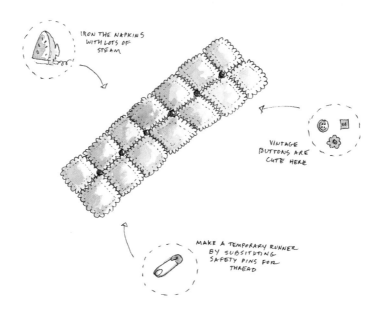

IRON THE NAPKINS WITH LOTS OF STEAM

VINTAGE BUTTONS ARE CUTE HERE

MAKE A TEMPORARY RUNNER BY SUBSTITUTING SAFETY PINS FOR THREAD

Sautéed Savoy Cabbage

*M*Y MOTHER HAS an irrational hatred of cabbage, and I grew up thinking it was something only Little Orphan Annie would eat. However, freed from the tyranny of my mother's house, I learned that cabbage is, well, delicious! Savoy cabbage is the green cabbage with the wrinkly leaves—it's the Shar-Pei of cabbages.

3 tablespoons olive oil

1 clove garlic, slivered

6 cups shredded savoy cabbage, washed and dried

½ cup good chicken stock

1 tablespoon white wine vinegar

1 teaspoon sea salt

2 tablespoons crème fraîche, or sour cream

1. Heat the olive oil over high heat in a large, deep-sided skillet, then drop in the garlic clove, swirling it in the oil until you can smell it, about 30 seconds. Add the prepped savoy cabbage all at once, poking at it and stirring until it begins to wilt, about 3 minutes more.
2. Reduce the heat to medium, add the chicken stock, vinegar, and sea salt, and cook, uncovered, for about 5 to 8 minutes, stirring now and then. Turn off the heat, check for salt, and add the bit of crème fraîche. Dish it up immediately.

TIME: *30 minutes*
FEEDS: *4, as a side dish*

CABBAGES, CABBAGES

*A*FTER I ESCAPED my mother's cabbage embargo, I discovered a whole world of excellent varieties I'd like to share with you:

GREEN RED SAVOY NAPA BRUSSELS SPROUTS

Salt-Roasted Root Vegetables

*R*OASTING'S A GREAT trick to give root vegetables big flavor, because the heat brings out and intensifies their natural sugars. The assortment of veggies here is just a guideline: add and subtract vegetables as you see fit.

1 cup coarse sea salt

A small bunch of thyme

2 large carrots, peeled and cut into large hunks

2 turnips, peeled and quartered

1 large parsnip, peeled and cut into large hunks

2 Yukon Gold potatoes, peeled and quartered

Drizzle of olive oil

1. Preheat the oven to 375°F. Spread the sea salt in a thick layer in a rimmed baking sheet or roasting pan. Separate the bunch of thyme and lay the sprigs evenly on top of the coarse salt.
2. Dot this bed with the vegetables, making a single layer. A little mist of olive oil on top should do the trick, and then into the oven.
3. Roast the vegetables for 35 to 40 minutes, until the carrots are easily pierced with the tip of a knife. Pick the roasted vegetables off the top of the sea salt and serve right away.

TIME: *Prep: about 15 minutes of peeling, then a bit under an hour, almost entirely unattended*
FEEDS: *4, as a side dish*

Care and Feeding of Grandma's Antique Silver

You might have, sitting around your house (maybe under your sink, or in the back of the linen closet) a few mismatched pieces of Grandma's silver, which might be a little Victorian for your taste. It's getting more Dickensian by the day, as it blackens and tarnishes, hidden behind your old sheets. Don't be so cruel! Old water pitchers or silver coffee urns are excellent repurposed as flower vases, and old candy dishes and the like make terrific wine coasters for the dinner table. So roll up your sleeves!

First, visit the local hardware store and get some silver polish. Ask for advice—if a certain *objet* hasn't seen the light of day in thirty years, it might need some extra-powerful TLC. Make sure you wear rubber gloves and an apron while you do this. Wipe the polish all over the silver using a very soft sponge—anything with texture will scratch and permanently ruin the metal. Then, running it under plenty of cool water, rinse away the polish. Repeat as many times as you need to. Dry the silver right away, using a dust cloth. Store the silver in bags specially made for that purpose (available at hardware and housewares stores) or, if the piece fits, in a resealable plastic bag, pressing out as much of the air as possible when you seal it.

Radicchio Salad

Naturally bitter, radicchio does well with a little softening—here, the runny yolk of a poached egg. The sunshine creaminess of the egg creates the balance necessary for a happy salad experience.

1 tablespoon cider vinegar

1 egg

1 head radicchio, washed, cored, and sliced thinly

1 tablespoon red wine vine

Sea salt

1. Bring a small pot of water to a steady boil, and add the cider vinegar. Break the egg into a large kitchen spoon or small dish, then lower the spoon into the water. Poach the egg for exactly 3 minutes.
2. Meanwhile, place the radicchio in a small serving bowl, and sprinkle it with the red wine vinegar. Lift the poached egg out of the water with a slotted spoon, drain it well, patting it gently with a paper towel, and lay it on top of the radicchio. Sprinkle on some sea salt. To serve, just poke a hole in the yolk and toss lightly.

Time: *About 10 minutes*
Feeds: *4*

DOGGIE BAGS

I am the queen of the restaurant doggie bag. It might be gauche, but I never finish my dinner and I have a constitutional aversion to letting good food go to waste, if it can be lunch tomorrow.

I fully support pressing leftovers on your guests, particularly such desserts as cookies or tarts, which can be easily transported and enjoyed another day. Just send them home with their goodies in either a chic shopping bag or in a brown paper bag, fastened with a brass paper fastener.

Chocolatey Floating Island

*T*HIS SUMMER, MY father made a chocolate floating island, and the poached meringue rested on a pond of chocolate crème anglaise. We decided that, while delicious, that incredibly rich chocolate crème anglaise was, well, too rich. So there's a trickle of chocolate in this floating island, but not a sea.

FOR THE CRÈME ANGLAISE:
2 cups whole milk
1 vanilla bean, split lengthwise
4 egg yolks
²/₃ cup sugar

FOR THE MERINGUES:
3 large egg whites
Pinch of salt

¹/₄ cup superfine sugar

FOR THE CHOCOLATE DRIZZLE:
¹/₂ cup sifted Dutch-processed cocoa powder
¹/₂ cup half-and-half
¹/₂ cup granulated sugar
2 tablespoons light corn syrup
1 tablespoon butter

1. Make the crème anglaise: Heat the milk with the vanilla bean in a medium-size saucepan just until it boils, then turn off the heat and cover the pan, letting the vanilla bean steep in the milk for 15 minutes.

2. Meanwhile, whip the egg yolks with the sugar until lemon-colored and ribbony, about 2 minutes. Add a ladleful of the hot milk, whisking briskly to prevent the eggs from scrambling, then pour in the rest of the milk, and mix to combine. Pour it (through a sieve) back into the saucepan, increase the heat, and cook it, stirring constantly, until it thickens, about 5 minutes. This won't seize up like a pudding, since there's no cornstarch in it, but it should give the back of your wooden spoon a nice gleam. Pour it in a bowl, cover tightly, and refrigerate for at least 4 hours.

3. Make the meringues: Put a large, clean kitchen towel on the counter next to your stove, and bring a wide, shallow pot of water to a simmer. Meanwhile, pour the egg whites into the bowl of your standing mixer and start them off slowly, breaking up the egg whites, and then increasing the speed and adding the salt. When the mixer is near top speed, and the egg whites are at stiff peaks, start adding the

superfine sugar in a very slow but steady stream over the side. You'll see the meringue turn shiny and pillowy. Beat the egg whites for 3 more minutes, until they are quite stiff.

4. Scoop out little dumplings of meringue—about a generous half cup's worth—and nudge them into the simmering water. It's handy to do this with two spoons, one to scoop, and the other to shape and nudge. You want to work a bit quickly, because the little darlings poach in no time. In fact, you want to give them about 1 minute per side—they will inflate magnificently—then fish them out and let them drain on your impeccable kitchen towel. When they're cool, transfer them to a sheet of parchment paper, cover lightly, and let them chill in the fridge.

5. Finally, the chocolate sauce: combine all the ingredients in a small saucepan over low heat, and stir until the sugar has dissolved and the chocolate is bright and shiny. You only want this warm not hot, so reheat very gently and briefly over minimum heat. Difficult, no?

6. Serving these is so fun, because everything is made ahead and it looks like you're whipping up a miracle for dessert. Set up four shallow soup bowls in a row, and pour a little lake of crème anglaise into each. Float two meringues in each lake, then drizzle a thin stream of the chocolate sauce over the tops (traditionally, this would be caramel). Serve, soaking up the oohs and aahs.

TIME: *About an hour of working time, though there will be a few pots and pans to wash. Make sure you leave several hours for the components to chill.*
FEEDS: 4

Well, Just a Touch
Dessert Wines and Digestifs

My father is a big one for bringing out the Baume-de-Venise, a lovely, sweet dessert wine served in tiny glasses. That bit about the tiny glasses is key—since dessert wines and digestifs are higher in alcohol and sugar than regular wine, they pack quite a punch. Two glasses is not recommended, if you'd like to avoid a headache.

However, if you want to dabble in digestifs, there are many sorts to choose from. Sauternes and other dessert wines can vary in color from buttercup yellow to amber, and go very well with citrus desserts. There are fortified wines, such as port. Then there are those that can blow your car doors off: eau de vie, for instance, or grappa. Alternatively, you can go for flavored liqueurs, like Sambuca, or Limoncello. The latter was the cause of thirty dollars worth of Enrique Iglesias songs being downloaded onto my iPod after midnight one night, so proceed with caution.

The Joy of Six

Potluck Principles

Having a potluck dinner is very Little House on the Prairie, but even if you don't wear a poke bonnet to yours, potlucks still serve up the same wholesome fun that they always did. Or maybe your potluck won't be so wholesome. I don't care—I'm not the wholesomeness police.

Good old-fashioned American values aside, the best part of a potluck dinner is that you don't have to be responsible for every last item your friends eat, but get to enjoy the pleasure of their company (and the fruits of their kitchen labor). In this case, I make you, the host, responsible for the main course, providing the drinks, and arranging the table. Your guests will have the pleasure of whipping up side dishes and desserts, which are more portable. Along with their assigned recipe, everybody should bring a cheapish bottle of wine, or beer, or whatever they might like to drink.

At the end of the night, you can gather around the fire, and listen to Pa play folk songs on the fiddle—no, wait, that's Laura Ingalls's night. At the end of your night, you can divide up the spoils and then go to another party.

THE TWO OF US . . . AND FRIENDS

Grandma Q's Meatballs

If EVER THERE was an old family recipe, this is it. Of course, it's not my family—people with surnames like Carry and Murphy rarely make the kind of meatballs anybody wants to eat. But my great-aunt Peggy made a good move dynastically: she married an Italian, my uncle Al. (He was also, appropriately, my godfather. Cue music.) And this is his mother's meatball recipe, the best meatball recipe of all time.

3/4 pound ground beef (preferably chuck)

1/4 pound ground pork

1 large clove garlic, finely minced

1/2 cup bread crumbs

1 egg

1/3 cup milk

1 teaspoon lemon zest

1/4 teaspoon ground cinnamon

1 tablespoon finely chopped fresh parsley

1/2 cup freshly grated Pecorino Romano cheese

1/2 teaspoon kosher salt

Pepper

1/4 cup olive oil

Aunt Peggy's Spaghetti Sauce (page 119)

1. If you use a butcher, have him grind the pork and beef together; if not, place them in a medium-size mixing bowl, and squish them together with your fingers. Add all the rest of the ingredients except the olive oil, and mix with your hands until just combined.
2. If you're going to eat the meatballs right away (see note), have a pot of the spaghetti sauce simmering in a medium-size saucepan on a back burner.
3. Heat the olive oil over medium-high heat in a large skillet. Form Ping-Pong–size balls, and roll them into the hot oil, turning them until they're nicely browned, about 5 minutes. Lift the meatballs out of the hot oil with a slotted spoon and slide them into the simmering sauce. Cook the meatballs for 35 minutes, until completely cooked through. Serve the meatballs and sauce over spaghetti (surprise!).

TIME: *About an hour, half unattended*
FEEDS: *Makes about 20 meatballs; figure 3 per person*
NOTE: *These meatballs are great freezer food. Instead of poaching them in the spaghetti sauce, drain the browned meatballs on a paper towel, then drop them in a freezer-strength resealable plastic bag and stick them in the freezer. They'll be good for 2 months. When you need them, simply finish the cooking in the spaghetti sauce, giving an extra 10 minutes to allow for defrosting.*

THE DAY AFTER

The Best Meatball Sandwich

YOU CANNOT MAKE Grandma Q's meatballs without saving a few to have a meatball sandwich. It's the law.

All you need is a nice Italian-style hero sandwich roll, some of Aunt Peggy's Spaghetti Sauce, and a lump of mozzarella cheese—for this, I like the Polly-O that comes shrink-wrapped, because it melts the best. First, split the roll and toast it lightly. Spoon some sauce on the bottom half, then add the meatballs, which you should slice in half first. Get as many as you can on there. Slice some mozz thinly, and drape over the top. Toast the bottom half in the toaster oven until bubbly and melted, then cap it with the top of the roll. Ohhh, I love meatball sandwiches.

Aunt Peggy's Spaghetti

ANOTHER FAMILY ALL-STAR, though I have tweaked it just slightly, reducing the amount of olive oil originally called for. It's a terrific basic sauce and so much better than the tinny stuff you get bottled at the supermarket.

1 (35-ounce) can highest-quality whole Italian plum tomatoes, such as San Marzano

¼ cup olive oil

1 large clove garlic, slivered

½ teaspoon kosher salt

½ teaspoon sugar

⅓ cup dry red wine

Pepper

1½ pounds spaghetti

Parmesan cheese, freshly grated

1. Zip the plum tomatoes around in the blender or food processor until they're pureed. Set aside.
2. Heat the oil and garlic together in a heavy-bottomed saucepan over medium heat, stirring constantly, until the garlic begins to turn golden (burning the garlic means starting again from scratch). Immediately add the pureed tomatoes and bring to a gentle boil. Add the kosher salt, sugar, wine, and pepper, to taste.
3. Cook, uncovered, at a very low boil, stirring occasionally, for 30 minutes, or until you can see the shininess of the oil on top of the sauce. Use immediately, or freeze.
4. Bring a pasta pot filled with water to a boil and cook the spaghetti according to the package directions. Drain, ladle several spoonfuls of the sauce over the top, then toss. Top the spaghetti with more sauce, the meatballs, and copious amounts of freshly grated Parmesan.

TIME: *About 40 minutes, but it is very low maintenance*
FEEDS: *Makes enough sauce for pasta for 6 (about 1½ pounds of spaghetti)*

The Basics
Potluck Organization

A few more thoughts about potlucking it up: It pays to be a bit organized. In the week before the dinner, hand out the recipes you want to use to the cooks they're best suited for—the people who never eat in, for instance, should perhaps be assigned the salad. If your friends have a definite opinion about what they want to make, yield gracefully. This is potluck, for heaven's sakes, not the Four Seasons.

In terms of table setting, you should be quite relaxed. Have several platters and bowls washed and ready to go when the dishes arrive, so you don't eat out of aluminum foil containers. Potluck is de facto buffet, so pile up some plates, and organize silverware into bunches—I like to use drinking glasses as impromptu vases for this purpose. With spaghetti, have plenty of napkins, and lots of country bread to wipe up the sauce.

Roasted Broccoli with Hot Pepper and Garlic

*T*HE BITE OF hot pepper and garlic in this dish makes the broccoli just as tasty at room temperature as it is fresh from the oven.

2 heads broccoli, trimmed and cut into large florets

3 cloves garlic, slivered

½ teaspoon crushed red pepper

¼ cup olive oil

1 teaspoon sea salt

1. Preheat the oven to 400°F.
2. Combine all the ingredients on a rimmed baking sheet, tossing them as you would a salad. Shake the pan so everything lies in a single layer, then add ¼ cup of water to the mixture.
3. Roast for 25 to 30 minutes, shaking the baking sheet once or twice, until the broccoli has turned crispy at the edges and cooked through completely. Spoon into a serving dish, taste for salt, and devour.

TIME: *45 minutes total, but only about 5 minutes work time*
FEEDS: *6, as a side dish*

POTLUCK ALTERNATIVES

*I*N KEEPING WITH the Italian-American theme, here are some possible substitutions:

LASAGNA   MANICOTTI   EGGPLANT PARMESAN

Arugula Salad with Pine Nuts and Golden Raisins

*T*HE RAISINS IN this salad give it a bit of a Sicilian twist.

¼ cup pine nuts	1 small clove garlic, crushed
¼ cup golden raisins	Sea salt and pepper
3 tablespoons red wine vinegar	6 cups arugula, washed, picked over, and dried (you can also use spinach here)
¼ cup olive oil	

1. Toast the pine nuts dry in a small skillet over lively heat, until they turn golden. You can also do this in your toaster oven. Set aside.
2. In an old, clean mustard jar, mix the raisins with the red wine vinegar, and let sit for 20 minutes. Add the olive oil and crushed garlic. Screw on the top the jar and set aside until needed.
3. When you're ready for the salad, open the jar, get rid of the garlic clove, and add sea salt and pepper to taste. Toss the arugula thoroughly with the dressing, then sprinkle the reserved toasted pine nuts on top.

TIME: *About 15 minutes, including washing and drying the arugula, the most boring kitchen job ever. I let JS do it.*
FEEDS: *Makes enough salad for 6*

Fennel Brittle

ONE WORD ABOUT making candy: it usually involves hot sugar. Nothing hurts as much as hot sugar coming into contact with your tender digits. So be careful. This recipe is inspired by the fennel seeds you chew on after an Indian meal to freshen your breath.

Nonstick cooking spray or vegetable oil	½ cup water
1 cup sugar	Pinch of salt
2 tablespoons light corn syrup	¼ cup whole fennel seeds

1. Prep a cookie sheet. First, hope that you have a nonstick sheet, because life will be easier that way. If not, coat a regular cookie sheet with a generous layer of nonstick spray or vegetable oil. If you have a nonstick sheet, it will still benefit from a lighter coating.
2. Pour the sugar in a small, heavy-bottomed saucepan, then gently pour the corn syrup and the water on top of it, poking at any large lumps of sugar with your finger so that the water moistens everything. Turn the heat on to medium-high, and let the sugar cook, boiling merrily, for 6 minutes. The syrup should crystal clear. Briefly take the pan off the heat and add the fennel seeds, all at once, not stirring. Return the mixture to the heat, wiping down the sides of the pot with a water-soaked pastry brush to avoid any crystallization. Cook for about 5 minutes more, until the sugar syrup turns a lovely light amber.
3. Immediately pour the sugar out on the prepared sheet, tilting the sheet this way and that to get a large, thin layer. Let it cool on a rack for 30 minutes.
4. Break the fennel into shards—some large, some small—and it's ready to serve.

TIME: *About an hour, 15 minutes when you actually have to do something*
FEEDS: *This makes as many shards as you'll need for a party of 6, with some left over. You can store it in an airtight container as long as you like.*

Candied-Orange Caramels

THESE ARE THE most laborious of the candies here, but a homemade caramel is a real old-fashioned treat. You'll need a candy thermometer for this recipe: though accomplished candy makers can use tricks like dropping doses of candy into a glass of water to see if the sugar is hot enough, for beginners there's no substitute for a thermometer's accuracy.

Nonstick cooking spray

¼ cup diced, candied orange peel

¾ cup light brown sugar

¾ cup dark brown sugar

3 tablespoons light corn syrup

Pinch of sea salt

¼ cup water

1 cup heavy cream

½ cup evaporated milk

¼ cup plus 1 tablespoon Grand Marnier or Cointreau

5 tablespoons butter, cubed

1. Prep the pan: Coat an 8-inch square cake pan with nonstick spray, then cut and line with an 8-inch-wide strip of parchment paper with longer tails on either end, like a table runner. Spray this well, too. Dot the bottom of the prepared pan with the candied orange peel, taking a minute or two to fuss with it so all the sticky little orange pieces are in an even layer.

2. Okay, now we're ready to cook. Combine the sugars, corn syrup, salt, and water in a heavy-bottomed medium-size saucepan, and bring to a boil over medium heat, swirling gently to help the brown sugar melt. Be a good anticrystallization policeman and brush the sides down with a brush soaked in water from time to time. When the sugar is dissolved and bubbling, insert the candy thermometer. It shouldn't touch the bottom of the pan, otherwise you'll get a false reading. Reduce the heat to medium-low, and cook, not stirring ever, for about 25 minutes, or until the sugar reaches soft ball stage, 238°F on that trusty thermometer.

3. While the sugar is heating, stick the heavy cream and evaporated milk in your microwave and heat for a minute or two, to take the chill off. It should be hot to the touch. When the sugar hits the magical 238°F mark, add the hot cream mixture in a steady stream, stirring the caramel all the while. Add 4 tablespoons of

the Grand Marnier, and then the cubed butter, a few cubes at a time. You'll notice that the temperature has dropped. Cook the caramel, stirring often, until the mix returns to 238°F.

4. When you've returned to temperature, whisk the pan off the heat, add the last dribble of Grand Marnier, and pour the caramel into the prepared pan. Let it sit at room temperature for an hour until cooled, then turn it out of the pan, peel of the parchment, and cut into scant 1-inch squares. Wrap these puppies in colored cellophane or waxed paper, or drop them into little paper candy cups.

TIME: *About 2 hours, half unattended*
FEEDS: *Makes about 60 tiny caramels*
SPECIAL EQUIPMENT: *You have to go splurge on a candy thermometer, which can also double as a deep-fry thermometer. I like the sort with the large dial gauge, rather than the more old-fashioned mercury ones. You will also need some waxed paper (or something prettier or more exotic) to wrap the finished caramels in, or they will stick to each other, and not just to your teeth.*

A TABLE MIRROR—SOMETIMES raised a bit on tiny feet so it's a plateau—is a time-honored way to reflect candlelight and make everyone feel more attractive around your dinner table. Old mirrors in nice frames can be rather expensive, but if you find an old cheapie on the street, you can tart it up to make an acceptable resting place for votive candles.

ARTISTIC TALENT METER: HIGH

YOU WILL NEED:

A small framed mirror, picked up at a home store, about 12 × 16 inches

Masking tape

A can of off-white spray paint

Old newspaper

Black acrylic paint

A small paintbrush with a thin tip

Elmer's glue

A 1-inch paintbrush

Several sheets of light pink or brown tissue paper, cut into strips

1. Take the mirror, the masking tape, the spray paint, and the old newspaper onto your fire escape or into your backyard, or another well-ventilated area. Fold a piece of newspaper to fit the mirror, and tape it down well with the masking tape, leaving only the cheap frame exposed. Lay down a few extra sheets of newspaper, lay the mirror on top, and spray paint that frame, two coats, letting it dry a bit in between. Let the frame dry completely before proceeding.

2. Using the black acrylic paint, scrawl a pithy food-centric saying around the rim of the frame. You could try "Tell me what you eat, and I will tell you what you are," from Brillat-Savarin, or "Avoid fried foods, which angry up the blood," from the immortal Satchel Paige. Let these words of wisdom dry completely.

3. Finally, make a soup of one part Elmer's glue to two parts water. Lay the strips of tissue paper over the frame one by one, completely saturating them with the glue. The tissue paper will turn translucent and let the saying shine through. After about 15 minutes, you'll be done. Let the glue dry completely, then peel off the covering over the mirror and plunk your new plateau in the middle of your table, dotted with votive candles.

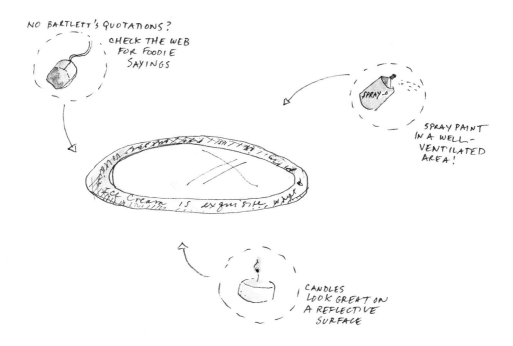

Cranberry-Cherry Chews

*T*HESE SHOULD ACTUALLY be called Cranberry-Cherry-Almond-Meringue Chews, but you'll be so busy chewing you won't be able to handle all those extra words. The tartness of the dried berries keeps these from giving you a sugar high-induced headache.

2 egg whites

½ cup superfine sugar

1 tablespoon cornstarch

½ cup dried cherries

½ cup dried cranberries

½ cup slivered, blanched almonds, lightly toasted

Zest of ½ lemon

¼ teaspoon almond extract

1. The trick of these chews is clever oven management. You need to preheat the oven to 300°F, then—as soon as you put the tray of chews in the oven—turn the oven down to 250°F. Do this and it will make you a master chew maker. So the first step is to preheat the oven to 300°F. Prepare a baking sheet by lining it with parchment paper, or use a Silpat, a very snooty-chef item that is like reusable parchment.

2. Set up your standing mixer with the whisk attachment. In an impeccably clean and dry mixing bowl, start breaking up the egg whites at slow speed. Gradually increase the speed, until you get stiff peaks forming. Have your sugar at the ready, and add it into the egg whites, in a very slow but steady stream, to make the meringue. Beat at high speed for 5 minutes, until it's an unbearably lovely shiny snow white. Take the bowl out of the mixer and stick a rubber spatula into it.

3. In a small bowl, coat the dried fruit and nuts in the tablespoon of cornstarch, and fold them into the meringue, making sure they're evenly distributed. Sprinkle the zest and the almond extract over the top, and fold again.

4. Using two teaspoons, drop little mounds of the chew mixture onto your prepared baking sheet. You can place them as close together as you like, as long as they're not touching. Slide the sheet into the oven, reduce the heat immediately to 250°F, and bake for 30 minutes. Don't peek. When your buzzer goes off, turn off the heat completely, and let the chews cool in the oven, at least 30 minutes. Take them out, and try not to make yourself sick by eating the whole batch at once.

TIME: *About 2 hours, but 15 minutes of actual cooking time*
FEEDS: *Makes about 50 candies*

Flower Power
DAISIES

DAISIES ARE A perfect potluck flower, cheerful and cheap as they are. The daisy's fatal flaw is its drippy fronds, which look rather unappealing in a glass vase. So, strip the leaves from the daisies as best as you can, then tie them up with a ribbon off an old birthday gift, and lay them on the table, next to the bunches of silverware and stacked plates.

The Food Critic
AKA THE COLOR COMMENTATOR

*S*ubject *can be* recognized by telltale expression: wrinkled brow, cocked eyebrow, and pursed lips, sometimes accompanied by finger poking of offending object. If particularly bold, subject will announce displeasure by making ostensibly neutral statement: "My, this risotto is very brown!" Overpowering the Food Critic involves wielding a firm smile and suggesting a taste of the offending dish, followed by a sweet assurance that it will be no trouble, you can whip something else up, if the dish is not acceptable. The shame will usually tame the Critic, who will eat (and enjoy) the same dinner as everyone else.

Six Cooks in the Kitchen Dinner

Seafood Fritto Misto (page 133)
Butternut Squash Risotto (page 136)
Tomato Pesto Salad (page 139)
Sweet Cheese Soufflés with Berry Coulis (page 142)

It's a fact of life that partygoers migrate to the kitchen, no matter how much money you spent on flowers for your living room. So if you can accommodate your friends in your kitchen, I say, why fight the inevitable?

At an average dinner party, you try to plan ahead so that you need to spend as little time as possible in front of the stove, which eliminates a whole host of culinary possibilities. But if you're eating at your kitchen counter, by your stove, you can play around with recipes that you would normally have to avoid. You're no longer saddled with sedate stews and legions of make-aheads. You can make it right now, damnit! And luckily, since they're just sitting there watching you, your friends can pitch in and help. Of course, you will couch this help in terms of "fun." After a glass of wine or two, they won't know the difference.

This menu features a trifecta of slave-to-stove favorites: Seafood Fritto Misto, which requires you to hover over a pot of hot oil; Butternut Squash Risotto, which requires you to stir diligently for twenty minutes; and Sweet Cheese Soufflés, which require the same amount of attention you have to give to a newborn child. But since the party has joined you, it's less work and more an ego-boosting showcase for your cooking prowess.

Party-Planning Time Line

DAY BEFORE:

BE HOUSE PROUD: Give your kitchen a good scrubbing, clearing off your countertops if people are going to be eating off them. Get out your prettiest bowls and make a few bowl covers (page 140).

AT THE BAR: Make sure you have some wine and beer on hand, along with a soft choice or two.

IN THE KITCHEN: Make the puree for the risotto, and the pesto for the tomato salad. You can also make and refrigerate the berry coulis.

DAY OF:

BE HOUSE PROUD: Take a few extra minutes and arrange your kitchen, including putting out piles of plates, glasses, knives, and forks.

IN THE KITCHEN: Prep the misto for the fritto misto and measure out the other ingredients; wash and arrange the tomatoes on a platter; measure out the ingredients for the risotto; and prep the ramekins and make the base for the soufflés.

DURING THE PARTY:

IN THE KITCHEN: While your guests help themselves to wine, make the batter for the fritto misto, then allow your friends to do for themselves. Start the risotto, and let people take turns stirring, while others slice the tomatoes for the salad. Finally, beat the egg whites and fold in the soufflé base for the soufflés. Watch with awe as they rise (fingers crossed) and have yourself a well-deserved glass of wine.

Seafood Fritto Misto

*A*NY DISH THAT translates into "mixed fried things" is a dish for me. There are as many variations of this Italian dish as there are shoe stores in Italy, some more exotic than others (fried beef testicle, anybody?). This seafood and veggie version, not including reproductive organs, lets your friends coat and fry their own choices.

GREMOLATA:

5 cloves garlic, minced

½ cup finely chopped fresh parsley

A large pinch of red pepper flakes, crushed

Zest of 1 lemon

Sea salt

FOR THE BATTER:

Vegetable oil, for deep-frying

3 egg whites

1½ cups all-purpose flour

1½ cups semolina flour

1 teaspoon kosher salt

FOR THE FRIED-THINGS-TO-BE:

1 pound medium shrimp, peeled, cleaned, and deveined

1 pound large sea scallops

1 pound small squid, cleaned and cut into large rings

1 lemon, cut into very thin rounds and seeded

12 shiitake mushrooms, wiped clean and trimmed

2 heads fennel, trimmed, cored, and cut into wedges

2 red or yellow bell peppers, cored, seeded, and cut into large strips

1. Well before dinner, you can make the gremolata topping: mix the garlic, parsley, lemon zest, red pepper flakes, and several hearty pinches of sea salt together in a small bowl. Set aside until needed.

2. Fill a medium-size saucepan with 3 inches of vegetable oil, rig up a deep-fry thermometer to the side of the pan, and heat the oil, over medium heat, to 330°F.

3. Meanwhile, whisk the egg whites in a large metal mixing bowl until light peaks form, about 5 minutes. You can also do this with a hand mixer, if your biceps aren't up to it (a hand mixer will beat the egg whites faster than you can). Mix the flour, semolina, and salt on a dinner plate and set the bowl and plate next to the stove. On the other side, cover a large platter with paper towels, or (which is cuter) strips of a clean old brown paper bag, to receive your well-fried bounty.

4. Arrange the fish and veggies nicely on a platter before you begin to fry them. Then in batches, as you need them, swipe the shellfish, the lemon, and vegetables in the egg whites, then coat them lightly in the semolina mixture. Fry until golden and cooked through, about 3 minutes or less. The easiest way to rescue these little treasures from the oil is with a bamboo-handled strainer, but a slotted spoon will do. Drain them on the paper, and sprinkle with the gremolata.

TIME: *About 30 minutes prepping the ingredients, and several minutes communal cooking time*
FEEDS: *6*
SPECIAL EQUIPMENT: *A deep-fry thermometer, which is also the same as a candy thermometer.*

The Basics
Kitchen Counter Eating

If you're going to have guests lined up at your kitchen counter or around a kitchen island, you need to set a bit of a scene—after all, this is dinner. First, a chair for each person is a must—during cocktail hour, people love to stand about, but it gets old once the main course rolls around. And though formal seating is perhaps overdoing it, mark places with wineglasses, a napkin, and a casual set of cutlery. Your friends will want to maneuver—sometimes helping you, sometimes not, but there should always be a place of their own where they can relax and enjoy the scene.

Butternut Squash Risotto

*F*ORGET ACORNS. THROW those spaghetti squashes away. The only squash worth lugging home from the market is the butternut, which boasts a sublime combination of taste, texture, and ease of cooking. The sweet earthiness of the squash goes very well with the starchiness of the rice, and the finished product, colored a delicate ochre, is beautiful to look at and wonderfully fragrant.

FOR THE PUREE:

1 medium-size butternut squash

2 sprigs rosemary

5 tablespoons unsalted butter

½ teaspoon salt

¼ teaspoon ground white pepper

¼ teaspoon ground cumin

FOR THE RISOTTO:

7 cups good quality chicken stock, simmering hot

1 tablespoon olive oil

⅓ cup finely chopped shallots

2 cups arborio or vialone nano rice

1 cup freshly grated Parmesan cheese

1 tablespoon butter

Salt and pepper

6 tablespoons finely chopped fresh parsley

1. Make the butternut squash puree. Preheat the oven to 350°F. Peel the butternut squash, then slice it in half lengthwise, scooping out and discarding the seeds. Put the squash cut side up on a rimmed baking sheet, put half a sprig of rosemary and a tablespoon of butter in each seed cavity, then sprinkle ½ cup of water in the bottom of the baking sheet and slide it into the oven. Bake the squash for 40 to 45 minutes, until there's good color on the squash and they're completely tender when pierced with a paring knife.

2. Cut the cooked squash into large chunks (set aside about ⅓ cup and dice it for serving), and place in the bowl of a food processor. You can discard the stems of rosemary. Pulse the butternut squash with the 3 remaining tablespoons of butter, salt, white pepper, and cumin, until it is uniformly pureed. Set aside.

3. Start the risotto: Make sure the chicken stock is simmering away on a back burner; then, in a heavy-bottomed saucepan, heat the oil over lively heat and

sauté the shallots for a minute. Add the rice, coating it in the oil, then add 1½ cups of butternut squash puree. Then, in ½ cup increments, stir in the hot broth, mixing continuously until the pot is dry, before adding another ½ cup. Continue cooking and stirring the risotto like this, for 15 minutes.

4. After 15 minutes, reduce the heat to medium-low and taste the rice. If it's still hard in the center of the grain, continue adding broth and stirring as you have been doing, for another 2 or 3 minutes. You may not end up using all of your stock. When you judge that your rice is almost perfectly done—not hard, but definitely not mushy—add the Parmesan, the lump of butter, and salt and pepper to taste. Ladle spoonfuls into shallow soup plates to serve, and top with a few chunks of squash and a pinch of chopped parsley.

TIME: *This takes over an hour, but the butternut squash puree can (and should) be made ahead*
FEEDS: *6, as a main course*

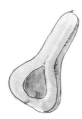

RISOTTO RICE

*T*HE MOST POPULAR of risotto rices, arborio is widely available now and is very versatile. However, it has the lowest amount of starch of all the risotto rices, and that's why it needs constant coaxing to release those starches and create that velvety sauce. There are two other rices, available in specialty Italian stores or high-end gourmet stores: carnaroli, which is quite delicate, and vialone nano, which, the starchiest of the bunch and can actually be more ignored, absorbs more stock at one time without turning into boiled rice, and thus is perfect for a dinner party, even one when you're eating right next to your stove.

RULES OF PITCHING IN

*H*ERE'S THE DEAL. This is dinner party with participation, and your guests will have a great time deep-frying their fritto misto and slicing up their tomatoes. But anything that's remotely a drag—chopping and washing vegetables, for instance, or grating Parmesan cheese, you should have done in advance and have close at hand for when you need it. It's fun to stir the risotto pot for two minutes—twenty, it's more of a workout.

Tomato Pesto Salad

*T*HIS IS SOMETHING to serve alongside the risotto, and is easy enough to give your guests as something to do while you stir your risotto. The perfect moment for this menu is late summer, as the squash is just arriving and the last great summer tomatoes are giving up the ghost.

A large bunch of basil

A small bunch of parsley

A small bunch of chives

¼ cup blanched almonds

⅔ cup olive oil

1 teaspoon sea salt

4 pounds assorted late-summer tomatoes, washed

8 ounces feta cheese, preferably preserved in oil, crumbled

1. Ahead of time, wash and dry the basil, parsley, and chives, and pick a few pretty leaves off from the basil to use as decoration later. Then, in a blender, puree the almonds with the basil, parsley, and chives. Add the olive oil in a steady stream with the motor running. Season with sea salt and taste, and correct seasoning.

2. Slice and quarter the tomatoes and arrange them on a platter in a few haphazard piles. Sprinkle the crumbled feta cheese on top. Then drizzle spoonfuls of pesto dressing over the whole salad and decorate with some basil leaves. So good, so easy.

TIME: *Without any help, 15 minutes, with help, 5*

FEEDS: *6*

SPECIAL EQUIPMENT: *A blender makes this a 5-minute salad.*

YOU DO IT
Bowl Covers

WHEN EVERYBODY IS in the kitchen, you have to make a concerted effort to keep the place from looking like Dr. Frankenstein's laboratory. You know, wipe down the counters, hide used bowls and utensils, and have your prepped ingredients—known in the biz as mise en place—chopped and separated neatly into bowls. For any bigger bowls that might need covering, consider making an old-fashioned bowl cover—it's a far sight more attractive than plastic wrap, and has the added bonus of being reusable, which is always a good thing.

To make them, I always use vintage dishtowels, particularly those with a stain or semi-unraveled ones. I cut away the offending parts, then use fabric glue to attach some rickrack or silly little ball fringe, picked up for a dollar at a trimmings store (again, a great online source for trimmings is mandjtrimming.com). If you're inclined to use something new, try going to a local imports store—both Mexican and Chinese variety stores have colorful, inexpensive tea towels that can be sacrificed for a bowl cover.

ARTISTIC TALENT METER: LOW

YOU WILL NEED:

A vintage or new kitchen towel

A felt-tip pen

A few yards of silly trim (rickrack, ball-fringe, beaded fringe)

Scissors

Turn a mixing bowl that you often use upside down on the kitchen towel, then trace a circle around the bowl, leaving a ½-inch clearance. Cut out the circle, then dot the edges with fabric glue. Work the trimming around the edge of the towel circle, pressing firmly. Let it be until the glue has dried.

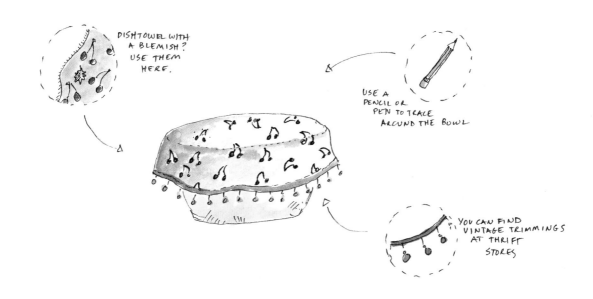

DISHTOWEL WITH A BLEMISH? USE THEM HERE.

USE A PENCIL OR PEN TO TRACE AROUND THE BOWL

YOU CAN FIND VINTAGE TRIMMINGS AT THRIFT STORES

Sweet Cheese Soufflés

 Soufflés HAVE A real *olé!* factor, but as a standard dinner-party dish they are a bit fussy. The fuss turns to fun if everyone is already in the kitchen. It's a kitchen science experiment, and very dramatic presentation.

3 tablespoons unsalted butter, plus several tablespoons for buttering the ramekins

3 tablespoons all-purpose flour

1¼ cup half-and-half

Grating of fresh nutmeg

Zest of 1 lemon

⅔ cup granulated sugar, plus extra for sugaring the ramekins

4 egg yolks

¾ cup farmer or whole-milk ricotta cheese

6 egg whites

1. Prep six 8-ounce ramekins: heavily butter, then sugar the ramekins. Set them aside until needed (if you've got a very hot kitchen going, stick them in the fridge).
2. Melt the 3 tablespoons of unsalted butter in a medium-size saucepan, then add the flour, stirring and mushing up any lumps. Cook over medium heat for 1 minute. Then, in a slow but steady stream, add the half-and-half, whisking continuously to prevent any lumps. Add the nutmeg, lemon zest, and sugar, and bring to a boil.
3. Meanwhile, beat the egg yolks in a separate mixing bowl until lemon-colored and ribbony. Add a ladleful of the hot half-and-half mixture, whisking all the while, then add the rest of the half-and-half. Let cool for a few minutes, then fold in the farmer cheese. Refrigerate until needed.
4. When you're close to baking time, preheat the oven to 375°F, and arrange the prepared ramekins on a rimmed baking sheet. In the very, very clean bowl of a standing mixer, start beating the egg whites, first slowly, then faster and faster, until they hold a stiff peak but don't look broken or dry. (For a little kitchen theater, you can always test their readiness by holding the mixing bowl upside down over your head. If the whites stay where they are, they're ready to go. If not, your guests will get a good laugh.) Mix a dollop of the egg whites into the cheesy souf-

flé base, then carefully and gently fold in the rest of the egg whites. Don't worry about perfect mixing, or you'll have perfectly flat soufflés.

5. Fill each ramekin to the brim, then wet your index finger and make a little ditch in the soufflé batter around the rim of the ramekin—this will help them rise. Slide them suavely into the oven, close the door with tact, and pretend your oven doesn't exist for 18 minutes. Then you can peek, just a crack of the oven door. If the soufflés are gorgeous examples of golden-brown goodness, pull them from the oven and impress everyone with your culinary prowess. If you need a bit more time, add a minute or two, but don't bake them for more than 20 minutes.

6. To serve, transfer the soufflés to plates, using a sturdy spatula and a pair of tongs. Serve with a spoonful of the Berry Coulis (see page 144).

TIME: *About 30 minutes active time*

FEEDS: *6*

SPECIAL EQUIPMENT: *You need six 8-ounce ramekins for this, but they're very inexpensive and will serve you well for many years.*

SOUFFLÉ 101

*T*HERE'S A GREAT scene in Woody Allen's *Love and Death* where Diane Keaton makes a soufflé that's so heavy it collapses their dining room table. Soufflés have a reputation for difficulty, but don't be intimidated.

For a dish that's so extravagantly showy, a soufflé is quite simple at heart. It's just a base, usually involving egg yolks, and the whipped egg whites, folded together and carefully baked. This is a dessert soufflé, but take out the sugar and you have a savory soufflé. Or, to look at it another way, remove the cheese and add ½ cup of crushed strawberries, or ½ cup of lemon curd, and you have a strawberry soufflé, or a lemon one. So break that soufflé barrier—once you do, you'll never look back.

Berry Coulis

WHEN YOU SERVE up the soufflés, take a spoon and knock a hole in the middle, and ladle a bit of this bright sauce inside.

1 pint raspberries, washed, a few set aside whole for serving

1 pint strawberries, hulled and chopped

½ cup sugar

½ vanilla bean, split

Squeeze of fresh lemon juice

1. Mix the raspberries, strawberries, sugar, and vanilla bean in a small saucepan with ½ cup water, and bring to a quick boil. Cook until the berries just begin to break down, 5 minutes. Remove from the heat and rescue the vanilla bean.
2. Pour the fruit into a blender, and whiz until pureed. Pour the puree through a sieve into a small bowl, pressing down on the contents of the sieve to get all the fruit you can. Add the lemon juice. Refrigerate until needed.
3. To serve, use a big spoon to make a divot in the top of each hot soufflé, and pour a few tablespoons of the puree into the center of the soufflé, and top with one or two raspberries. Eat up.

TIME: *Less than 15 minutes*
FEEDS: *Makes 2 cups of sauce*

Most Wanted
the Early Bird
AKA MRS. PUNCTUALITY

Subject is so excited to be at dinner, that he rings the doorbell five minutes before the time they were invited for, while host is only wearing one sock and hostess is frantically trying to wrestle several unsightly items—a laundry bag, two shoe boxes—under the bedskirt. Awkwardness ensues as host makes hearty chitchat while buttoning his shirt and the hostess hides in the back trying to put on some undereye concealer. How can you deter the dreaded Early Bird? Tell subject that the invite is for *seven forty-five*, if everyone else is invited for seven thirty and, not being early birds, will probably begin arriving at seven forty-five. Early arrival solved.

Seat-of-Your-Pants Gourmet

Smoked Salmon Salad with Dill and Crème Fraîche (page 147)
Duck Confit Ragout with Pappardelle (page 152)
Pan-Roasted Artichoke Hearts (page 155)
Cheese
Easy Chocolate Fondue (page 157)

There's a moment when you can see quite clearly that you're headed for disaster. In the recent past, during a spurt of bonhomie, you invited for dinner those nice people you met at so-and-so's wedding. Then your brother wants to come, so you invite him, and he wants to bring someone, too. Then, all of a sudden, it's five o'clock on Friday afternoon, dinner's at eight, you're in the supermarket frantically grabbing ingredients, and you realize that you never made your bed this morning, and the dishwasher is full of dirty dishes because you forgot to run it.

What do you do? You make a run for the deli counter and pray that you can scrounge together a fantastic, quick-to-prepare meal from what you can find there. And never fear: you can. The trick is just not making dinner seem like a glorified frozen dinner, so that means no premade main courses, or lumps of pâté with a few gherkins for a first course. A little ingenuity, however, and you will have a completely creditable dinner to feed your friends.

Smoked Salmon Salad with Dill and Crème Fraîche

*T*HIS IS REALLY a *salade composée*—very little work to do except arrange this prettily on a platter so others can attack it.

1 head romaine lettuce, preferably pre-washed

1 pound smoked salmon

3 tablespoons chopped fresh dill

2 scallions, white and light green parts only, sliced

Zest and juice of 1 lemon

1 cup crème fraîche or sour cream

Sea salt and pepper

1. Separate the romaine lettuce into spears, and arrange them, cupped side up, on a large platter. Drape pieces of smoked salmon in the cups so that the salmon would stay put if someone were to pick it up and eat it.
2. Sprinkle the dill and the scallions over the top of these little romaine lettuce barques.
3. Mix together the lemon zest, lemon juice, and crème fraîche in a small bowl (or even in the crème fraîche container). Add lots of freshly ground pepper and a pinch of salt. Drizzle the dressing over the top of the salmon, and voilà! First course.

TIME: *About 5 minutes, if you don't need to wash the romaine*
FEEDS: *6*

Quick Reference
Party-Planning Time Line

TWO HOURS BEFORE:

BE HOUSE PROUD: Do a quick once-over of the bathroom and living area; close doors to rooms your friends don't need to see.

AT THE BAR: Stick some white wine in the freezer, and set your timer for 45 minutes—at the buzzer, transfer the wine from the freezer to the fridge.

IN THE KITCHEN: Start the duck confit ragout by chopping and prepping the ingredients, then getting them cooking. Wash the lettuce if it's not prewashed. Preheat your oven.

ONE HOUR BEFORE:

IN THE KITCHEN: Have your pasta pot full of water and ready to go. Assemble the salmon salad and stick it in the fridge. Throw the bits and pieces of the artichokes in a roasting pan and slide them into the oven. Arrange a platter of dried fruit for the dessert. Check the ragout—it should be done and just left on the stove to reheat later.

HALF AN HOUR BEFORE:

BE HOUSE PROUD: Turn on some tunes and turn down the lights. If need be, turn them way down.

AT THE BAR: Open a bottle of red, and set out a few glasses.

IN THE KITCHEN: Plate the various predinner treasures you've come up with. A longer, heartier cocktail hour will give you time before dinner needs to be on the table.

AT H-HOUR:

AT THE BAR: Put out any refrigerated beers and wine.

IN THE KITCHEN: Take the artichokes out of the oven and turn on the heat to medium under the pasta water. Let your friends linger over drinks, then bring out the salad, family style. Turn the heat on under the ragout.

DURING:

IN THE KITCHEN: Throw the pasta into the pot, then, during the cheese course, make the easy fondue.

DELI NIBBLES

SNATCHED OFF THE rack in moments, these tried-and-true tidbits can give your guests enough to eat while you stall for time making dinner:

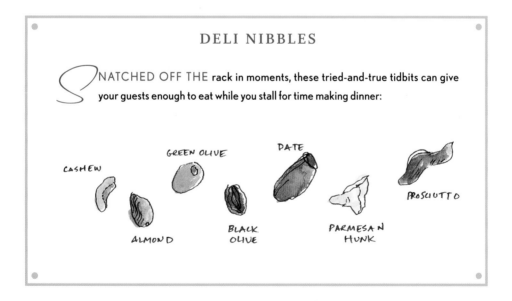

CASHEW

GREEN OLIVE

DATE

PROSCIUTTO

ALMOND

BLACK OLIVE

PARMESAN HUNK

Care and Feeding of Candleholders

I've used lots of items not originally intended as candleholders for candle-holders—candy molds, cheese drainers, lemons (see page 80), and juice glasses, just to name a few—but I've also used my fair share of real candleholders and candlesticks. And sometimes, I've even bothered to clean them.

If it's a dark and stormy night, a rusty candelabra with lots of drippy wax can be quite romantic and beautiful. But otherwise, sometimes those crusty candlesticks could use a bath. There are two state-sanctioned methods: first, to bake the candlesticks upside down on a cookie sheet lined with parchment paper in a low oven for several hours, so that the wax melts out; or second, to pry the wax out with a knife you don't care about, then running the holders under boiling water to melt the waxy residue.

If you have glass holders, give them a good wipe down with white vinegar after-ward, drying them with an old T-shirt. That way, they'll be sparkling for the next time you need them.

Prettifying Prepackaged Food

There are two ways of attacking prepackaged food. The first is the easier: choose items (fancy cocktail biscuits, for instance) that spend as much money on the containers as they do on the contents. They look fancy and imported, and the packaging is part of the fun, particularly if there's a seal from the British royal family or something.

Most everything else—pâtés, spreads, dips, dried sausages, smoked fish—can be mixed up, fluffed up, trimmed, and decorated to look like something much more impressive. When things come in plastic containers (hummus, for example), I decant it into a clean screw-top jar that's lost any original provenance it might have had. With some nicely arranged toasts laid out on a dinner napkin, and sprinkled with a bit of paprika and a drizzle of olive oil, it looks casual and fun—but not store-bought. Just remember—plastic is never attractive!

Duck Confit Ragout with Pappardelle

$\mathcal{R}$AGOUT IS ONE of those things that takes hours of careful braising, conscientiously monitoring the pot and tasting repeatedly so as to find the perfect flavor balance. Well, that's what's in television ads, at least.

In this case, we're in a hurry, dammit, and there are people arriving any minute and I still don't have any mascara on. So this is ragout, express.

The duck confit is something that any gourmet store should carry, where you can buy it by the leg. The beauty of confit is that it's completely cooked and ready to go, so this recipe just heats it up and makes it into a sauce. If the confit proves elusive, you can use shredded rotisserie chicken legs and thighs, instead.

1 carrot, peeled and cut into chunks

1 onion, peeled and roughly sliced

3 cloves garlic

2 tablespoons vegetable oil

2 tablespoons tomato paste

2 cups button mushrooms, sliced

2 confit duck legs and thighs, skin and bones discarded, meat shredded

Several sprigs fresh thyme, or 1 teaspoon dried

½ cup white wine

1 cup beef broth (bouillon cube encouraged)

2 tablespoons butter

Salt and pepper

1½ pounds dried pappardelle noodles, or the widest egg noodles you can get your hands on

Handful of chopped fresh parsley

1. Absolutely pulverize the carrot, onion, and garlic in your food processor, if you have one. If not, chop them as finely as you can, particularly the carrots. Heat the oil in a large skillet with a lid, and dump the vegetables in all at once, adding a pinch of salt and ½ teaspoon of freshly ground pepper—this should have some zip. Sauté over medium-high heat for 5 minutes, until the onion is translucent.

2. Stir in the tomato paste, then add the mushrooms, shredded duck confit, and the thyme. Give the dish a quick stir, then add the wine and the beef broth. Cook over very low heat, lid slightly ajar, for 20 to 25 minutes.

3. As the sauce cooks, bring a huge pot of water to a boil and add a fistful of kosher salt. Using the directions on the pasta package, time the pappardelle so that it finishes cooking at the same time as the sauce—it will usually take about 10 minutes. (Alternatively, you can make the ragout earlier and just reheat it for dinner.)
4. After 25 minutes elapses, take the cover off the ragout, raise the heat to medium, and swirl in the butter. Drain the pasta very well and add it to the skillet, turning with tongs (salad servers are also very useful for this job). Top with oodles of the chopped parsley and serve it up.

TIME: *About 30 minutes*
FEEDS: *6 as a main course*
SPECIAL EQUIPMENT: *Your sanity will be much enhanced by a food processor.*

Centerpieces
Odd Logic

When you're setting a table, no matter what you're using, remember these principles of grouping:

Either, one big statement . . .

or five
items grouped
in two-three
formation . . .

  . . . or three smaller ones

. . . or a march of seven items down the table.

Pan-Roasted Artichoke Hearts

ARTICHOKES ARE ONE of the great pleasures of life, but they can be time-consuming. However, there are wonderful people who sell artichoke hearts in a box, which you can find in your friendly neighborhood freezer section. These are little treasures you can gussy up with few ingredients and almost no attention paid.

¼ cup olive oil

3 cloves garlic, slivered

2 (10-ounce) packages frozen artichoke hearts, thawed

½ teaspoon kosher salt

1. Put the olive oil and garlic in a cold skillet, and heat gently for several minutes, until you can really smell the garlic. Meanwhile, if the artichoke hearts are whole, saw them in half, lengthwise. When the garlic is garlicky, toss the artichokes in the oil, along with the salt.
2. Cook, covered, over low heat for 25 minutes, until the edges of the artichokes are crispy and golden. Taste and correct for salt, and serve right away.

TIME: *About 30 minutes*
FEEDS: *6, as a side dish*

Cheeses

SOMETIMES, ALL THOSE mysteriously wrapped cheeses at the deli counter hiding all taste and smell behind industrial plastic can leave you guessing. Which ones will taste good? Which ones will taste just like the plastic they're wrapped in?

In my experience, avoid any soft cheeses, other than young goat cheeses, which you can roll in herbs and lemon rind yourself when you get home. Otherwise, stick with hard and semisoft cheeses, such as smoked Gouda and real Cheddar and Muenster. You'll get the most real cheese flavor that way.

CHEDDAR   GOUDA   GOAT

Easy Chocolate Fondue

THIS DESSERT IS easy, because you don't need some sort of kitschy fondue kit to make it. In fact, all chocolate fondue is easy. Cleaning it out of your tablecloth after dinner is hard.

THE FONDUE:

1¼ cups heavy cream

¼ cup granulated sugar

3 bars (3½-ounce) of high-quality semi-sweet chocolate

1 tablespoon kirsch or other liqueur (optional)

1 tablespoon unsalted butter, softened

THE FRUIT:

½ cup dried figs, halved

½ cup dried apricots

½ cup dried pears

½ cup walnuts

1. Pour the cream and the sugar in a small saucepan. Turn on the heat, looking for the tell-tale little bubbles around the edge of the pan.

2. Meanwhile, break up the chocolate bars by beating them up with a rolling pin, or can of tomatoes, or what ever bludgeon you have hanging around. When you see those bubbles in the cream, give the cream a stir and make sure the sugar has dissolved, meaning you shouldn't feel the granules with the back of your spoon. Take the cream off the heat, unwrap the chocolate, and pour the shards into the hot cream. Stir continuously with a wooden spoon until the chocolate is completely melted, about 3 minutes. Until it is totally smooth, it will look like a terrible mess. Just keep stirring.

3. Finally, add the optional booze and the butter and stir it in. Use immediately, served with a platter of the dried fruit and nuts and some fun cocktail toothpicks, or those things you use to hold corn (why not?).

TIME: *10 minutes*

FEEDS: *Ample for 6, after dinner*

CARNATIONS ARE THE ultimate last-minute flower—you can find them anywhere, and they come in all sorts of colors, including some hilariously fake ones: smurf blue, for instance, or St. Patrick's Day green. You can't take a bouquet of carnations seriously, so go for the craziest ones you can find: just make sure that they're all the same color. Mass the carnations very tightly, and bind them first with a rubber band, and then some ribbon or twine, to hide the rubber band. Cut them off quite short. I like to use a tumbler for them, or old scented-candle glasses that I've sent through the dishwasher. If you have time, do several vases full, at least three, because with carnations, there's power in numbers.

*D*o *you see* this table? Six people had lots of fun here. From the look of it, too much fun. But instead of giving up and setting that tablecloth on fire, try these get-clean-quick schemes:

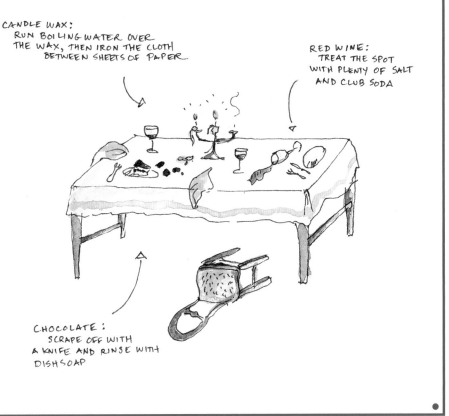

CANDLE WAX:
RUN BOILING WATER OVER
THE WAX, THEN IRON THE CLOTH
BETWEEN SHEETS OF PAPER

RED WINE:
TREAT THE SPOT
WITH PLENTY OF SALT
AND CLUB SODA

CHOCOLATE:
SCRAPE OFF WITH
A KNIFE AND RINSE WITH
DISHSOAP

The Great Outdoors

JS and I never seem to make it out of the city on the Fourth of July. While everyone else is somewhere picturesquely patriotic, we're on the steamy streets of Manhattan. One year, having not planned anything in particular, I decided to throw a last-minute celebratory picnic. Location? The roof of our building, easily reached by climbing the fire escape out our bedroom window. JS transported several ratty tablecloths and a Moroccan lamp up to the roof (note to the nice firemen at Engine Company 5: the flame was watched at all times) and we had ourselves a very urban picnic with several friends, hearing the boom of the Central Park fireworks in the distance, and admiring the red-white-and-blue light scheme on the Empire State Building.

Eating outside in the summer is always preferable, but there's something extraordinarily pleasant about pretending to rough it in the grass (or on the tar paper), even when you are surrounded by delicious tidbits to eat and all the proper utensils. This menu, rather than being the American cliché, is Mediterranean in bent, with lots of yummy dips and a great North African-inspired main course, perfect at room temperature.

Quick Reference
Party-Planning Time Line

WEEK BEFORE:

BE PICNIC PROUD: If you're feeling crafty, stitch up a reusable, waterproof picnic blanket (page 172)

DAY BEFORE:

BE PICNIC PROUD: Wash off any old coolers or baskets that will be making the trip with you.

AT THE BAR: Buy any cheap picnic wines and other drinks you like, and put them in the refrigerator to chill. Check your supply of ice packs for traveling.

IN THE KITCHEN: Make the skordalia, taramasalata, and baba ghanouj. You may poach the fish for the b'steeya the day before, too. Finally, make the apple tartlets, which can cool in the oven overnight.

DAY OF:

BE PICNIC PROUD: Assemble your collection of outdoor-worthy utensils and plastic plates, along with a cutting board, ice packs, a serrated knife and corkscrew, salt and pepper, a trash bag, and anything else that seems useful, dividing things equally so the weight is shared by all.

AT THE BAR: Keep your drinks in the fridge for as long as possible before leaving the house.

IN THE KITCHEN: Assemble the b'steeya, bake it, then refrigerate it until you're ready to go. Lastly, make the parsley salad.

Skordalia

$\mathcal{S}$KORDALIA IS A garlicky, hearty Greek meze, or starter. You can make this with stale bread or with potatoes. As an Irish-American, I plead guilty to the potato stereotype.

1½ pounds of Yukon Gold potatoes, boiled, peeled, and cooled

¼ cup plain Greek yogurt

3 tablespoons extra-virgin olive oil

Juice of ½ lemon

3 large cloves garlic, grated

2 tablespoons finely chopped fresh parsley

1 tablespoon finely chopped fresh mint

Sea salt and pepper

1. Smash the cooled potatoes well with a potato masher or the back of a fork. Mix in the yogurt, olive oil, lemon juice, grated garlic, and herbs, and add salt and pepper to taste.
2. Refrigerate until you serve it, but it tastes best at room temperature. Serve with pita crisps.

TIME: *About 30 minutes, including potato-boiling time*

FEEDS: *6, with other dips*

Mediterranean Cheats and Substitutions

Don't bother to make pita chips for your dips: just pick up a bag of them, making sure they're not dusted with some artificial mélange of flavors: there's plenty of real garlic here to make any garlic powder unnecessary and unwanted. If you can't find this easiest of cheats, just cut up several pitas with your kitchen scissors. You can toast them or not, depending on your taste and patience.

I've included three dips here that I swear by, but many other options are open to you at a high-end deli counter. Tzatziki and hummus are obvious substitutions, and, if you have time to make only one or two of these, you can cheat by picking up the others at the store.

PURCHASED PITA CHIPS

SAYID'S SPREADS!
STORE-BOUGHT HUMMUS

GREEK PRIDE
DELI-MADE TZATZIKI

The key here is starting time—even with summer's long evenings, you're going to want to head out with your picnic gear at a reasonable late-afternoon hour: you want to eat at sunset, not in the dark.

Lugging the appropriate gear around is another point worth discussing. You'll need an insulated pack for the food, another for drinks (wine and bubbly water), and then a basket for all the gear—the picnic blanket, a cutting board, a knife, the basic dining utensils, plastic plates and glasses, a corkscrew, and a discreet trash bag to keep things nice and neat. It might be easier to have everyone meet at your house, or at least arrive at your picnic destination together, so that the heavy lifting can be evenly distributed among friends.

Finally, lay out all the food all at once—picnics are ultimately about grazing and feeling you have more choices to eat than could fit on your plate.

Taramasalata

TARAMASALATA IS ANOTHER hearty Greek meze perfect for dipping pitas in. The main ingredient is tarama, a preserved fish roe. Before you flip the page, let me try to convince you that tarama is pretty easy to find in the supermarket's international foods aisle, and the finished product is creamy, smoky, salty, and pink! (all right, it's really coral). Not that I play favorites, but if I were to make just one of these three dips, it would be this one.

4 thick slices country bread, preferably day-old, crusts removed

Juice of 1 lemon

2 shallots, minced

2/3 cup tarama (carp roe)

1 cup extra-virgin olive oil

1. Soak the bread in 1 cup of warm water for 30 minutes, then squeeze it dry. Put the soaked bread in the bowl of a food processor with the lemon juice, shallots, and tarama. Pulse until combined, then, with the motor running, add the olive oil in a slow stream until completely emulsified.
2. Scrape the taramasalata into a small bowl, and cover tightly. Refrigerate for several hours or overnight before serving.

TIME: *Mere minutes' prep time, but leave time for the taramasalata to refrigerate.*

FEEDS: 6

RAIN DATE SOLUTIONS

ABSOLUTELY DON'T TREK somewhere with all your food and equipment if there's even a chance of rain—soggy pita chips make a sad tableau. I always think it's fun to have a picnic, even if it's in the middle of your living room. If you insist, you can always sit on chairs (or the couch) but mimicking your outdoors plans indoors will make people laugh.

Baba Ghanouj

I JUST LOVE saying "baba ghanouj," putting a bit of mustard on the last syllable: ghanoujjjjjjj! Apart from my lunacy, this eggplant-based Middle Eastern dip is garlicky good, and healthy, besides.

2 large eggplants (about 3 pounds)

3 cloves garlic, 1 slivered, 2 minced

¼ cup plus 3 tablespoons extra-virgin olive oil

⅓ cup freshly squeezed lemon juice

½ cup tahini (sesame seed paste)

1 teaspoon ground cumin

1. Preheat the oven to 300°F. Pierce the eggplants all over and slip a few slivers of the garlic into the incisions. Rub the eggplants with the 3 tablespoons of olive oil, and slide them into the oven on a rimmed baking sheet.

2. Bake the eggplants for 1 hour, turning once, until they have collapsed slightly. Let them cool on the counter, then cut off and discard the tops, peel them by pulling off the skin, and hack the flesh into bits. Transfer them to the bowl of a food processor.

3. Blitz the eggplants for a moment, then add the minced garlic cloves, the ¼ cup of olive oil, and the lemon juice, tahini, and cumin. Whiz.

4. Scoop the baba ghanouj into a bowl, and cover tightly. Refrigerate until picnic time.

TIME: *About an hour, mostly unattended, plus refrigeration time*
FEEDS: *6*

The Pink and the Green:
INEXPENSIVE PICNIC WINES

I'm not advocating public drunkenness or open containers outdoors, but at the same time I'm not a policeman and I think you're crazy if you don't lug along a little something to make the evening pass smoothly.

Since picnicking is a quintessential summertime exercise, I suggest reaching for some wines you wouldn't drink at any time of the year. The first is rosé. Now, I say put down anything called "blush zinfandel" that comes in a box, or any rosé wine made in Hungary, Romania, or Canada, but some rosé from the south of France or from California is perfectly respectable, and more fun than some dreary old white.

When I say "green," I mean verde—vinho verde, low-priced Portuguese wine that has a slight effervescence to it. Vinho verde, which seems to have endless producers, should never cost you more than $10 and comes in pretty, slender, green-tinted bottles. Château Latour it ain't, but it will work admirably for a summer picnic. Just remember to encase it in a picturesque crumpled brown paper bag.

B'steeya de Poisson

$\mathcal{B}$'STEEYA IS A Moroccan-style tart, usually made with chicken, flavored with almonds and a hint of cinnamon sugar and encased in golden, flaky phyllo dough. In the summer, switching to a firm white fish such as cod makes it lighter.

I'm not going to give you a song and dance about how you can whip this up in fifteen minutes while doing your nails simultaneously. You can't. But it's delicious and unusual, and really, will take an hour of kitchen concentration for a spectacular picnic dish.

TO COOK THE FISH:

1 bay leaf

6 peppercorns

1 shallot or small onion, peeled

Several sprigs of fresh parsley and cilantro

1/2 cup white wine (optional)

2 pounds firm white fish, such as halibut
    or cod

FOR THE FILLING:

2 large, ripe tomatoes

1 cup blanched and slivered almonds

3 tablespoons confectioners' sugar

1 teaspoon ground cinnamon

3 tablespoons unsalted butter

3 tablespoons all-purpose flour

1 1/2 cups whole milk, heated but not boiling

Pinch of saffron threads

1/2 teaspoon kosher salt

Pinch of cayenne pepper

3 egg yolks

1/2 cup chopped fresh parsley

1/4 cup chopped fresh cilantro

Sea salt

1 (1-pound) package frozen phyllo dough,
    thawed

1/4 pound (1 stick) butter, melted

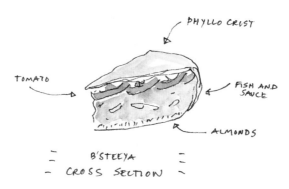

PHYLLO CRUST

TOMATO

FISH AND
SAUCE

ALMONDS

B'STEEYA
CROSS SECTION

1. Cook the fish: Fill a medium-size saucepan halfway full with cold water, and add the bay leaf, peppercorns, shallot, herb sprigs, and a slug from the white wine bottle you have open in your fridge (this is optional, but adds great flavor). Bring this to a boil, and let it boil for 10 minutes. Add the fish, and regulate the heat so that the water is just simmering—this should really be a hot bath for the fish. Cook, prodding the fish occasionally, for about 15 minutes, or until the fish is completely opaque (this time is approximate because the thickness of your fish will determine its cooking time). When it's finished, lift the fish out of the broth and let it cool on a plate. Bring the broth back to a boil.

2. Prepare the tomatoes: Drop the whole tomatoes into the broth, and let them roll around for 30 seconds. Pull them out, turn off the heat, and discard the broth. Peel the tomatoes (that was the purpose of blanching them) and cut them into slices at least ½ inch thick. You want to have at least eight thick slices. Push out and discard the seeds, and set the tomatoes aside.

3. Now the almonds: Toast the almonds in your toaster oven or in a pie plate in your oven until lightly golden—moderate heat should do it. Blitz them in your food processor with the confectioners' sugar and cinnamon until crumbly.

4. Finally, the béchamel sauce: In a medium-size saucepan (can be the same one you cooked the fish in, cleaned) melt the butter. When the foaming subsides, add the flour and stir vigorously for 1 minute over lively heat. Slowly add the hot milk (I usually heat the milk in the microwave, but you can heat it in a small saucepan on the stovetop) and whisk until the mixture comes to a boil and thickens, about 5 minutes. Turn down the heat to low, and add the saffron threads, the kosher salt, and cayenne pepper. Finally, whisk in the egg yolks one at a time, stirring continuously until they're all combined. Take the béchamel off the heat and add the chopped herbs. Taste for salt and set aside to cool. Flake the now cooled off fish into large pieces, and add it to the béchamel sauce and set aside.

5. Preheat the oven to 375°F.

6. Line a rimmed baking sheet with parchment paper, and spray it with the cooking spray. Next, it's time to face the phyllo. Unroll the package of phyllo, and immediately cover the exposed sheets with a damp kitchen towel. Lay sheets of phyllo on top of each other, brushing each with butter, at a 45° angle from the

last one, so that you get a phyllo dough circle. Use about eight sheets to do this. After you've built up your layers, brush the whole lot with butter. Keep the unused pile of phyllo dough covered at all times with the damp towel.

7. Sprinkle the almonds in an 8-inch circle on your buttered layers of phyllo, then spoon the fish and béchamel mixture on the top. Finally, top this with the rounds of tomato, sprinkling them with sea salt. Fold up the edges of the phyllo dough to make the sides of the pie. Now, take several more sheets of phyllo, brushing each with butter, and lay them on top of the tomatoes, tucking the edges underneath the pie, making a neat package. You'll want to use at least six sheets of phyllo this time, to make sure everything is well encased. Brush the top with the remaining butter, and slip the pan into the oven.

8. Bake for 20 to 25 minutes, until the top is golden brown and the phyllo is crispy. Let the b'steeya cool in the pan for 15 minutes, then lift it off carefully using two spatulas and a bit of patience. This is most easily transported in a cake box or a small pizza box. Though it's best at room temperature, you should refrigerate it if you've made it this far head of dinnertime.

$\sim$

TIME: *An hour or more of working time, plus an hour for baking and cooling*
FEEDS: *6, for dinner*

Parsley Salad

OH, PARSLEY. IT'S crisp and clean. My grandmother used to eat it all the time because she said it made her breath fresh, even back when she was smoking unfiltered Chesterfields. Behold the power of parsley, or the power of self-delusion.

2 bunches of flat-leaf parsley	1 shallot, minced
1 bunch of watercress	5 tablespoons olive oil
2 tablespoons white wine vinegar	Sea salt and pepper

1. Wash and dry the parsley and watercress, cutting away their stems as much as possible. Don't go crazy, but do spend about 5 minutes picking through the bunches—it's the tender leaves we want, not fibrous stems.
2. For picnic purposes, put the parsley and watercress together in a resealable plastic bag, or a plastic salad bowl with a lid. To make the dressing, combine the white wine vinegar with the shallot, olive oil, and salt and pepper to taste in a small jar with a tight-fitting lid. Combine the salad with the dressing right before you want to eat it.

TIME: *10 minutes, salad washing time*
FEEDS: *6, as a side dish*

Picnic Blanket

IT MAKES SENSE, if you're considering picnicking more than once or twice, that you make yourself a real picnic blanket, so blankets that you actually use in the course of your life—ones that keep you warm in your bed in the winter, for instance—stay nice and clean, and grass- and wine-stain-free. There's no need to add a dry-cleaning bill to your budget for this party.

So what to use? I suggest a sheet, with a little clever waterproofing. Any standard full sheet will do, from an old set of your mother's, or from the local thrift store. It's more fun if it's not white, but if it is, bring a permanent pen and people can write little notes to you on it, sort of like your own personal graffiti.

I will say this is the first of several YOU DO ITs that involve a sewing machine. If you don't have one, your Aunt Tillie surely does, and she's more than happy to give you a crash course. This sort of sewing calls for the same amount of skill as a chimpanzee hitting a coconut with a rock, so know you can do this, even if you've never sewn before.

ARTISTIC TALENT METER: MEDIUM

YOU WILL NEED:

A standard full sheet, the prettier the better

A cheap, clear plastic shower curtain, standard size

Tape measure or ruler

Pencil

Scissors

Straight pins

A sewing machine

1. Spread the sheet, top side down, on your living room floor (or any place you have enough room). Using the tape measure, get the size of your sheet—double sheets tend to be about 75 × 95 inches, but measurements vary depending on manufacturer, so it's worth a quick check. You want to make a square, so, in the case of the standard sheet, snip off about 20 inches from the length of the sheet.

2. Lay the shower curtain on top of your sheet square, smushing out any folds and helping it to sit flat. Shower curtains are 72 inches square, so you should have a 72-inch-square on top of a 75-inch square. Fold the edges of the sheet over the shower curtain, and pin it all around, folding the corners so everything looks neat.

3. Now, head over to your sewing machine. If you're feeling particularly daring, you can thread the machine with a contrasting color. Feed one corner of your sheet into the machine, and, following the lines of your pins, choose a zigzag stitch, and let 'er rip. Sewing the whole thing should take less than 10 minutes.

4. Turn the sheet over, so that the fabric side faces up, and you'll see a pretty, waterproofed sheet, perfect for dining al fresco.

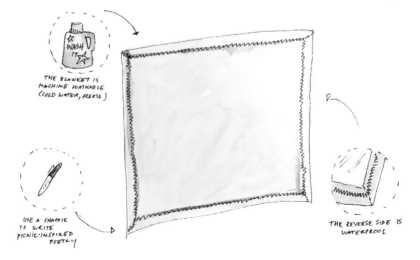

THE BLANKET IS MACHINE WASHABLE (COLD WATER, PLEASE)

USE A SHARPIE TO WRITE PICNIC-INSPIRED POETRY

THE REVERSE SIDE IS WATERPROOF

No-Crust Apple-Almond Tartlets

*T*HESE ARE LIKE big chewy apple cookies. The trick is to bake them for a while at a low oven temperature, and use an apple with some integrity—no McIntoshes (or other sauce apples) here, please! You'll only get mush.

4 Gala or Fuji apples, cored and peeled

¼ cup honey

1 tablespoon fresh lemon juice

1 tablespoon butter, melted

¼ cup raw almonds, chopped coarsely

1. Preheat the oven to 275°F. Slice the apples horizontally into ⅛-inch rounds, so, if you were so inclined, you could spin a disc on your finger like a LP. Prepare a sheet pan by lining it with parchment paper or by using a Silpat, if you have one.
2. Mix the honey with the lemon juice and melted butter in a small bowl, and have a pastry brush at the ready.
3. Assemble the tartlets: Lay out a slice of apple, brush it with the honey mixture, and place another apple slice on it, overlapped like a flower petal. Brush that one, and continue. You want a tight circle of apples, four or five slices per tartlet.
4. Sprinkle the tartlets with a hearty pinch of the chopped almonds, then slip the pan into the oven and let the apples bake for two hours. Turn off the heat and let the pan cool in the oven. Store in an airtight container, separating the tartlets with squares of parchment or waxed paper.

TIME: *Several hours, mostly unattended*

FEEDS: *Makes 6 to 8 tartlets*

SPECIAL EQUIPMENT: *An apple corer, for the prettiest tartlets*

Care and Feeding of Travel Kits

These picnic items, which you pull out of your closet after several months away, will often have turned an interesting yellow and acquired a strange smell if you don't do more than just rinse them clean when you get home. A few tips:

INSIDES OF INSULATED CONTAINERS (THERMOS, COOLER): Scrub the insides of these items with a bit of baking soda, to take away any lurking odors and stains.

HOMEMADE PICNIC BLANKET: This can actually be laundered in cold water, then hung up to dry. Just use gentle detergent—no bleach. Alternatively, a spritz of countertop spray will work to clean the plastic underside.

BLUE ICE PACKS: Wash them off before refreezing, and make sure they lie flat in the freezer. Though they look indestructible, after a while they might leak if frozen into weird shapes, wedged in between your Eggos and that package of Gardenburgers.

Eight and Up

Dinner Party, Capital D

Oysters Rockerfeller-ish (page 180)
Carrot Soup with Miso (page 184)
Veal Stew with Chives, Dill, and Pearl Onions (page 186)
Baked Red Wine Basmati (page 188)
Endive Salad with Honey-Yogurt Dressing (page 189)
Ice-Cream Sandwiches (page 192)

There comes a time in every host or hostess's life when you have to roll out the real napkins and serve up a dinner that is stylish and elegant. It goes without saying that the hostess has to do this in high heels, and without excessive swearing at the stove and/or her significant other.

If you're a free spirit, this kind of party might initially seem like an endless maze of lists and timetables. It's true that you do have to be prepared, conscientiously making ahead those things that can be made ahead, and taking a bit of time to think about setting the table and who will sit where. But just because there's some structure to an evening, doesn't mean that it won't be fun. No matter how old you get, throwing a fancy dinner party still feels like dress-up, and everybody, save the biggest sticks in the mud, likes to play dress-up now and again.

Party-Planning Time Line

ONE DAY BEFORE:
BE HOUSE PROUD: Make sure you have enough napkins, forks, clean glasses, etc., on hand. Give your bathrooms a once-over.

AT THE BAR: Shop for wine, beer, and sodas.

IN THE KITCHEN: Make the ice-cream sandwiches, the carrot soup, and the veal stew.

DAY OF:
BE HOUSE PROUD: Set the table and organize the seating.

AT THE BAR: Make sure what should be in the fridge (beer, white wine, soda) is in the fridge.

IN THE KITCHEN: In the afternoon, prep the salad components, but don't dress the salad until it's needed. Cook the rice and keep it at room temperature, ready to go under the broiler. Assemble the oysters and refrigerate them, ready to go under the broiler.

RIGHT BEFORE:
BE HOUSE PROUD: Set up cocktails, putting out nuts and olives for your friends to munch on. A bit of low music and some nice lighting is a good idea.

IN THE KITCHEN: Gently reheat the soup and the stew over low heat. Warm up the broiler, and throw in the rice before you sit down for the first course. Other than dressing the salad, everything is now ready when you need it.

Oysters Rockefeller-ish

$\mathcal{R}$EAL OYSTERS ROCKEFELLER are a bit Mamie Eisenhower-esque. However, they are worth an update because they make a spectacular presentation and are really, really tasty.

1 (1-pound) box kosher or coarse sea salt

16 oysters, shucked by your friendly neighborhood fishmonger

3 strips bacon

¾ cup fresh bread crumbs

1 cup watercress, washed, picked over, and chopped coarsely

1 teaspoon chopped fresh tarragon

3 scallions, white and light green portions only, sliced thinly

A drizzle of Pastis, Ricard, or Pernod

Salt and pepper

1. Preheat the oven to 500°F. Fill a roasting pan with the salt. Cushion the oysters (in their shells) in the salt, and set aside for a moment.

2. Cook the bacon in a large skillet over low heat until crispy. Crumble the bacon and set aside, and pour off all but 1 tablespoon of the bacon fat. Throw the bread crumbs into the remaining fat, and toss over medium heat for a minute or two, until lightly toasted. Take off the heat and stir in the watercress, tarragon, and scallions.

3. Return to the oysters. Top each oyster with a pinch of crumbled bacon, then with a spoonful of the bread crumb mixture. Drizzle a few drops of Pastis over the top of each oyster.

4. Bake the oysters for 10 to 12 minutes, until the bread crumbs are browned and the oysters are cooked through. Serve them warm, on a bed of salt, if you like.

NO PEARL INSIDE

TIME: *About 20 minutes*
FEEDS: *Makes enough for 2 oysters per guest*

OTHER UPSCALE NOSHES

*I*F YOU WANT to break the bank, you can always eschew oysters and go for some caviar, served on water crackers with some grated egg. You don't need mounds of it, since a little goes a long way. You could always serve it in a Buddha-shaped ice sculpture, as Auntie Mame does, but maybe that would be over the top. (However, I would love to reintroduce ice sculptures. All I would need is a chisel and some talent.)

Another simple option is some very high-quality Nova smoked salmon on thinly sliced rye toast points served with capers, shallots, and freshly ground pepper. The best smoked salmon in the world comes from Murray's Sturgeon Shop in New York, and they'll ship some to you (Murray's Sturgeon Shop, 212-724-2650).

PATÉ de FOIS GRAS

The Basics
Dinner Time Lines in Depth

Though an evening should never feel like a forced march, you do need to make an effort to at least sketch out a time line, particularly since you have food that will be past its prime if you sit down at ten, rather than eight thirty.

If you can, consider setting the table and dealing with centerpieces and flowers the day before, as well as doing most or all of the shopping. Getting the dessert done the day before is a plus, giving the ice-cream sandwiches plenty of time to set up. On the day of, make the soup, and then the stew. Have the rice ready to be baked, and the oysters ready to go when people arrive, so all you need to do is pop things in the oven and gently reheat stews and soups on the stove. The salad, so simple, can be made *à la minute*. Finally, remember to take the ice-cream sandwiches out of the freezer and let them soften a bit in the fridge before serving them—fifteen minutes should do it.

As for guests, invite people for seven thirty, expecting them to show up fifteen minutes late. That way, you can plan on sitting down at eight thirty, with the soup already at each place as your friends make their way to the table. The most important thing is not to rush—every recipe here can stay indefinitely in a low oven or over low heat on the stove, so there's no panic about a few minutes here and there.

And one last thing: though your friends will probably lend a helping hand on the wine front, make sure that you can cover dinner, in case everybody brings you lilies instead. Generosity is the word of the day.

Channeling Emily Post

PLACE CARDS AND OTHER PROTOCOL

Seating arrangements might seem like something from another century, but it's lots easier to have some idea where people might sit, so that your friends don't hang about uneasily playing musical chairs. Make a seating chart, doing your best to alternate men and women. There's some debate about splitting up couples, but I'm a firm believer that Lucille can speak to Frank when she gets home, so she doesn't have to at my dinner party. Place cards are optional but nice. Or you could always call out places from a master list, auctioneer style.

Carrot Soup with Miso

EVERYBODY ALWAYS MAKES carrot soup with orange juice, and it's good, but it always tastes like orange juice. But carrot soup is so pretty, and so easy, that it's a perfect dinner party dish. I was futzing around in the kitchen trying to avoid the orange juice, and I came up with this.

1 tablespoon vegetable oil	1/4 cup rice
1 large onion, chopped finely	8 cups very good-quality chicken stock
1-inch piece fresh ginger, peeled and left whole	3 tablespoons miso paste
2 1/2 pounds carrots, peeled and cut into large hunks	Scallions, sliced on the diagonal, for serving
	Sea salt and pepper

1. Heat the vegetable oil in a soup pot, then add the chopped onion and the whole chunk of ginger, along with a generous pinch of salt. Sauté over medium heat until the onions sweat and relax, about 5 minutes. Add the carrots and rice, and toss to coat them in the onions, then add the chicken stock and miso paste, throw in another pinch of salt, and cook, uncovered, for 30 minutes, at a very lazy boil.
2. When the carrots are tender to the point of falling apart, try to find and discard the little round of ginger. Then puree the soup in your blender, food processor, or food mill until it's smooth. Taste and correct for salt and add some good gridings of pepper. Serve hot, topped with a few green ovals of sliced scallion.

TIME: *About an hour, mostly unattended*
FEEDS: *8, as a first course*

SEASONAL INGREDIENT SUBSTITUTIONS

*T*HIS MENU IS an evergreen, meaning you can make it whenever and the quality will remain the same. But if it's high summer, you can replace the carrot soup with Gazpacho with Almonds (page 88), or the Avgolemono Soup with Mint (page 233). The veal stew is a miracle of simultaneous heartiness and lightness, and you could add some torn basil leaves at the last minute, if basil is bountiful. Also, the basmati rice could be augmented with a few roasted cherry tomatoes, and the endive salad could include whatever salad greens catch your fancy in the market. But don't touch the ice-cream sandwiches. They are perfect, year round.

Veal Stew with Chives, Dill, and Pearl Onions

THIS IS A version of a blanquette, which is a white stew as opposed to a brown one. It's more dinner-party friendly, and those little pink morsels of veal are as tender as can be—you don't even need a knife.

32 pearl onions (about a pound)

2 tablespoons vegetable oil

4 ounces pancetta or bacon, cut into matchstick-size pieces

¼ cup all-purpose flour

4 pounds veal stew meat, well trimmed, cut into 1½-inch cubes

½ cup dry white wine

2 cups chicken stock

¾ cup heavy cream

¼ cup chopped fresh dill

¼ cup snipped fresh chives

Juice of ½ lemon

Salt and pepper

1. First, deal with the pearl onions. Set aside a bowl. Bring a small pot of water to boil, then drop in the pearl onions, skin and all-this is the best way to peel them. After 3 minutes, drain and run under cold water to cool them off. Cut off both root and top, and give 'em a squeeze, aiming at the bowl you've set aside for this purpose. The skinned pearl onion will shoot out. When you're finished peeling, set the onions aside.

2. Salt and pepper the veal liberally; put the flour on a dinner plate or shallow bowl. In a heavy casserole—the cast-iron enamel ones are best here—sauté the pancetta in the oil over medium heat until it is lightly browned. Then add the veal, lightly dredged in flour, browning in batches so as not to crowd the pan. Don't worry about deep color—a light gold is what you're looking for here.

3. Return all the veal (and any juices) to the casserole, then add the wine. After it has boiled furiously for a second, add the chicken stock. Bring the pot back to a boil, then reduce the heat to a minimum, cover the casserole tightly, and let cook for 45 minutes.

4. When the buzzer goes off, add the pearl onions to the stew and uncover, raising the heat a bit so that you see a few lazy bubbles rising to the surface.

5. After 20 more minutes, add the heavy cream, chives, dill, and lemon juice, and stir to combine, tasting for salt. Let simmer for 10 more minutes for the flavors to come together; you can serve it right away, or you can make it ahead (which has an added bonus of letting the flavor develop) and reheat it very, very gently before serving.

TIME: *Several hours; about 45 minutes of working time, the rest mostly unattended*
FEEDS: *8 elegant diners*

MULTIPLICATION TABLE
Smaller Stews

IF STEW FOR four is what you're after, halve the amount of veal and the vegetables, but use the following amounts of liquid: $1/2$ cup heavy cream, $1 1/2$ cups chicken stock, and $1/4$ cup white wine.

Baked Red Wine Basmati

*T*HE ADDITION OF red wine makes ordinary basmati rice extraordinarily rich in flavor, and beautiful on the plate.

2 tablespoons unsalted butter	2 cups dry red wine
1 shallot, finely chopped	½ teaspoon kosher salt
2½ cups basmati rice	Parsley, chopped, for garnish

1. Preheat the broiler.
2. Melt 1 tablespoon of the butter in a medium-size saucepan, then add the shallot, and give it a good stir until a bit translucent, 1 or 2 minutes. Add the rice, and swish it around in the butter. Pour in the wine, plus 1½ cups of water, and the bit of kosher salt. Bring the pot to the boil, then cover, reduce the heat to a minimum, and cook for 14 minutes.
3. You now need a shallow casserole dish that won't get angry in the broiler. Dump the rice into the dish, smooth out the top with a spatula, then butter the rice with the remaining tablespoon of butter. Broil for 5 minutes, until the top dries and turns crispy and brown.
4. To serve, spoon out portions, making sure you get some crispy top for everyone. A few flecks of parsley livens the whole thing up.

TIME: *10 minutes of working time, then about 20 minutes of unattended time*
FEEDS: *8, as a side dish*

Endive Salad with Honey-Yogurt Dressing

$\mathcal{E}$NDIVE IS A staple of wintertime salads, but it's delicious and bracingly bitter year-round. There's just a hint of honey to brighten up the yogurt dressing.

¼ cup plain Greek yogurt

2 teaspoons honey

Juice of 1 lemon

Sea salt and white pepper

6 large endives, washed and sliced crosswise into ½-inch rounds

1 tablespoon finely chopped fresh tarragon

1. In a large salad bowl, swish the yogurt together with the honey and lemon juice. Add sea salt and pepper to taste.
2. Toss in the endive slices, turning them around in the dressing for a full minute so that every piece is evenly coated. Sprinkle with the tarragon and serve.

TIME: *Less than 10 minutes*

FEEDS: *8, with cheese*

WINEGLASSES

$\mathcal{D}$ON'T LIKE REGULAR wineglasses, or don't have enough to go around? Try these:

FRENCH BISTRO GLASSES

COLORED-GLASS JUICE GLASSES

CRYSTAL STEMLESS GLASSES

Painted Tablecloth

✂

THIS PROJECT INVOLVES a little imagination, and a small investment in table linen and acrylic paint. However, it's a foolproof way to make a cheapo thrift-store tablecloth look like a rare find. Where to get the art supplies? I say pearlpaint.com, or your local art supply store.

When it comes to what you want to paint, look about for inspiration: Moroccan floor tiles? Indian tapestries? Japanese flower paintings? Pennsylvania Dutch motifs? Have a bit of fun with this. I've sketched out a leafy sample for you to consider.

ARTISTIC TALENT METER: HIGH

YOU WILL NEED:

A few photocopied motifs that you would like to repeat

Thin cardboard or oak tag

A pencil

Scissors

A plain cloth tablecloth that fits your table, washed, dried, and well pressed

A thin and a thicker (½-inch) natural-bristle paintbrush

Acrylic paint, in one color or two complementary colors

Acrylic gel medium (this is for texture)

A paper plate or other makeshift palette

1. First, get your templates in order. Whatever picture you've found, copy it, enlarging it and reducing it so you have it in several sizes. Cut out one image, then trace the outline onto the cardboard. Cut out the template, being careful to make the edges as smooth as possible. Repeat with the other sizes.

2. Lay out the tablecloth, and start playing with the templates, working from each corner. When you're happy with placement, trace the template and move on. The pencil tracings can be erased and repositioned until you're happy. When you're ready to paint, decide if you want everything in the same color, or the occasional flower, bird, or leaf in a different color. Next, mix your paint with a bit of acrylic gel medium, so that it's nice and slippery, but you don't need to use any water. Using the small brush, paint over the outlines you've traced with the pencil. Then fill in the middles with the larger brush. I don't want to crush your natural artistic expression, but you should try to stay within the lines.

3. Let the tablecloth dry completely before moving it to your table.

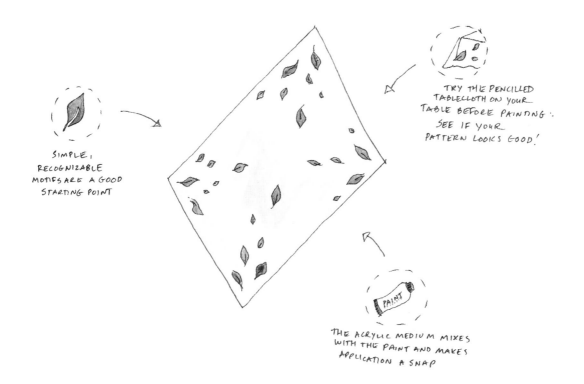

SIMPLE, RECOGNIZABLE MOTIFS ARE A GOOD STARTING POINT

TRY THE PENCILLED TABLECLOTH ON YOUR TABLE BEFORE PAINTING. SEE IF YOUR PATTERN LOOKS GOOD!

PAINT

THE ACRYLIC MEDIUM MIXES WITH THE PAINT AND MAKES APPLICATION A SNAP

Ice-Cream Sandwiches

THE PERFECT COOKIE for an ice-cream sandwich—and this is a scientific fact—has to have enough heft to deal with the ice cream, but can't freeze into a solid block, or be so crispy that it breaks as soon as you bite into it. Clearly, this is one of the greatest problems in ice-cream sandwichdom. But using a recipe of my Nonna's—with some strategic alterations—I think I've cracked the code.

FOR THE COOKIES:
¾ cup solid vegetable shortening
¾ cup light brown sugar
¼ cup light corn syrup
1 large egg
1 teaspoon vanilla extract
1 cup all-purpose flour
½ teaspoon baking soda

½ teaspoon salt
¾ cup quick oats
1 cup mini semisweet chocolate chips
½ cup toasted pecans, well chopped

TO ASSEMBLE THE SANDWICHES:
2 pints good-quality vanilla ice cream
(if you're so inclined, make your own)
1 cup white, coarse crystal, decorative sugar

1. Preheat the oven to 375°F. Grease some cookie sheets.
2. In a large mixing bowl, cream the vegetable shortening with the sugar and the corn syrup until light and fluffy. Add the egg and vanilla, and mix until combined.
3. Sift the flour, baking soda, and salt together, and stir into the creamed sugar mixture. Then fold in the oats, chocolate chips, and pecans.
4. Drop heaping tablespoonfuls onto the greased cookie sheet, leaving ample room to let these puppies spread. Bake for 12 minutes, and whisk them out of the oven when they are set and the edges just turn the slightest gold. If you overbake them, you'll miss the elusive chewiness necessary for perfect ice-cream sandwich enjoyment. Lift them off the cookie sheets and let them cool on a rack.
5. At least 2 hours before you want to eat these guys, take the vanilla ice cream out of the freezer and let it soften.

6. Now for the rocket science part of the meal: spoon a heaping spoonful of ice cream on one cookie, and top with another. Tidy it up and make it look pretty, then roll the edges in the sugar for a little crunch. Let the sandwiches firm up in the freezer for at least an hour before serving.

TIME: *30 minutes or so of working time, and several hours of freezer time*
FEEDS: *Makes 8 to 10 excellent ice-cream sandwiches*

Tablescapes, by Season

If flowers are a snore, try these tabletop ideas:

SPRING: Try arranging the many pretty young onions, leeks, and garlic shoots, together on a wicker tray.

SUMMER: Eggplants of all colors, squiggly shapes, and sizes make a striking tableau.

FALL: Lugging home several tons of squash makes sense when you see how pretty it looks in the middle of your table.

WINTER: Branches of brussels sprouts are unusual looking, and can scare your guests into thinking you're actually going to feed them brussels sprouts.

ARRANGE SPRING
ONIONS

PLACE SUMMER
EGG PLANTS

A FALL SQUASH
TABLEAU

WINTER: BRUSSELS
SPROUT BRANCH

The Impossible Dream: Dinner for 16

My friend Weatherly and I have a history with dinner parties. When we were twelve, we dressed up in two of her mother's old bridesmaid's dresses, burdened the dining room table with enough china for a royal state dinner, and had a very soigné meal of broccoli and beef stew by candelabra candlelight.

This moment of silliness was not the last.

Years later, Weatherly hosted a dinner party at her parents' house, when she was out of college and they were out of town. The guests numbered at least fourteen, and while we were setting the table, we indulged ourselves by putting out every random utensil found in her mother's vast silver drawer. Sauce spoons? Check! Fish knives? Check! Each person had at least four goblets and glasses at his or her place, and there were silver napkin rings and place cards. The stage was elaborately set for a blowout dinner party. Earlier in the day, Weath had made her way to the local market and picked up a huge slab of salmon and some egg noodles, along with salad greens and several tons of ice cream. The idea was to roast the salmon, toss the noodles with butter and parsley, have a bit of salad, and then top it off with an ice cream free-for-all. Unfortunately, as the guests started arriving, so did many bottles of champagne, and as the clock started ticking toward ten, and the collective volume kept rising around the table, it became clear that Weatherly had forgotten the dinner part of dinner party.

That much alcohol and that little food was a recipe, all right: a recipe for disaster. So I took matters into my own hands. Enlisting Weatherly's younger sister as sous-chef, I threw that salmon into a 500°F oven, boiled up those noodles, and served them with orange and lemon zest (Weatherly had forgotten the parsley, but had plenty of citrus for mixed drinks). Like Henry Ford, I set up an assembly line, recruiting a few more guests to dole out portions. By ten fifteen, dinner was on the table. I will allow that Weatherly looked a bit surprised when her plate was plunked down in front of her.

To protect yourself from turning into Weatherly, it makes sense to do two things: cook before you've had more than one glass of wine, and plan to cook ahead. With so many people arriving, you'll have to play host, not chef. This menu fits that bill, and it has an added saving grace: the main course can be served buffet style. It saves a lot of ferrying of plates in and out of the kitchen, even if you have Weatherly's little sister as your sous-chef.

Parmesan Cheese Crisps

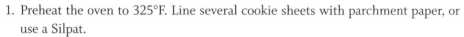

QUICK AND EASY, these make a great salty cocktail treat. They can be made days ahead and kept in an airtight container.

1½ cups freshly grated Parmesan cheese

½ cup freshly grated Pecorino Romano cheese

1 teaspoon cracked pepper

1. Preheat the oven to 325°F. Line several cookie sheets with parchment paper, or use a Silpat.
2. Mix the three ingredients in a bowl. Then, make little mounds of cheese, 2 or 3 tablespoons each, spaced apart so they won't melt into each other as they're baking.
3. Bake for 25 minutes, until the Parmesan crisps are completely melted and lightly golden. Let them cool on the sheets for at least 15 minutes—they must become crisps, after all—then transfer them to a serving dish lined with a nice napkin.
4. Optional snooty step: Using a spatula, while the cheese is just out of the oven, lay the crisps-to-be over your rolling pin or jar of olives—you get the idea—and leave them there until cooled. If you do this, they are no longer ho-hum cheese crisps, they are cheese tuiles. Very fancy.

TIME: *About 30 minutes*
FEEDS: *Makes about 25 crisps*
SPECIAL EQUIPMENT: *For optional shaping, a rolling pin or slim jar.*

Quick Reference
Party-Planning Time Line

TWO DAYS BEFORE:

BE HOUSE PROUD: Give your place a good cleaning and see if you need to borrow any plates or utensils; check for platters; make place-saving napkin rings (page 204).

IN THE KITCHEN: Make the Parmesan cheese crisps.

AT THE BAR: Make sure you have enough vino and nonalcoholic substitutes on hand.

ONE DAY BEFORE:

BE HOUSE PROUD: Set the table, ironing anything that needs to be ironed. Give the bathrooms a once-over.

IN THE KITCHEN: Make the pissaladieres, and wrap them in plastic wrap when they're completely cool. Clean and dry the salad. Make the chocolate cake.

At the bar: Buy ice.

DAY OF:

IN THE KITCHEN: In the morning, marinate the lamb, and prep the cauliflower. In the afternoon, roast the cauliflower, and in the late afternoon, the lamb. Chop the herbs for the couscous.

RIGHT BEFORE:

BE HOUSE PROUD: Set the mood with some flattering light and groovy music. Set out some pistachio nuts and your Parmesan crisps.

AT THE BAR: Set up a little bar with wine and beer, plus nonalcoholic extras. Uncork some wine in anticipation of dinner.

IN THE KITCHEN: Pull the lamb from the oven, and tent it with foil. Arrange the pissaladieres on plates and have the salad and dressing ready to go.

DURING:

IN THE KITCHEN: Dress the salad and top the pissaladieres right before serving. Warm the cauliflower in a 250°F oven. Heat the stock and make the couscous. After the first course, grab a friend or several friends and carve the meat, arranging it on the platter. Fluff the couscous and add the herbs. Spill the cauliflower into a serving bowl.

At the end of dinner, whip the cream, then cut the cake. Relax!

Most Wanted
The Overimbiber

AKA THE COCKTAIL HOUR HURLER, THE TIPSY TALKER

Subject is most notable for helping himself one too many times during cocktail hour, without taking a moment to line his stomach with as much as a cashew nut. Telltale characteristics include boisterous laughter, circular arguments, and a slight list to one side.

What can you do to avoid the Overimbiber? Be vigilant. Cocktail hours should in fact be cocktail half hours. It's your job to feed your guests. Chances are, once the first course is served, the Overimbiber will surrender to relative sobriety.

THE TWO OF US . . . AND FRIENDS

Care and Feeding of Linen Napkins

White linen napkins are lovely, and very satisfying resting in your lap during dinner. However, they can be a bit pesky when it comes to making them look as nice as they did when you first brought them home from the store. Here are a few hints:

First, to get stains out, wash them in very hot water, with strong detergent. These new detergents with oxygen are very useful here. If you live in a sunny climate, you can soak them in lemon juice and water, and hang them out to dry—they'll be bright white that way.

Once they're washed, throw them in the dryer but try to collect them before they're like the Sahara, because they will be easier to iron if they're still moist. Of course, I always forget to do this. So, when it comes to ironing them, have a spray bottle of fresh water, a can of spray starch, and a good iron with lots of steam. This is the process: Spritz the napkin with water, then with spray starch. The fabric should feel damp. Then, wrestling a bit with the napkin so there's some tension in the linen, press the napkin, using ample steam to really get that sucker to obey. Fold the napkin, and press flat again. Wipe your damp brow and continue with the next napkin.

Store napkins together, flat, tied with string, or, if they're small enough, in a resealable plastic bag, to keep them pristine for when you next need them.

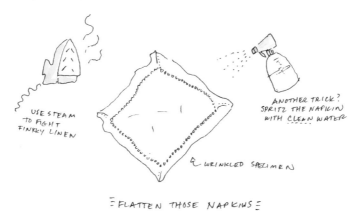

USE STEAM TO FIGHT FINICKY LINEN

ANOTHER TRICK? SPRITZ THE NAPKIN WITH CLEAN WATER

A WRINKLED SPECIMEN

= FLATTEN THOSE NAPKINS =

Pissaladiere and Salad

$\mathcal{A}$ PISSALADIERE IS a Provençal-style tart with four main ingredients: dough, onions, olives, and anchovies. If you use, use one of my favorite cheats in this recipe—a prepared pizza dough—the only ingredient that needs any cooking before the tart is baked is the onions. Pissaladieres are perfect at room temperature, and can be made the day before. The salad should be dressed right before serving.

FOR THE PISSALADIERES:

15 large onions, peeled and sliced into thin half-moons

¼ cup olive oil

¼ cup unsalted butter

1½ teaspoons kosher salt, plus more to taste

Pepper

1 small bunch of thyme

2 packages premade pizza dough (enough dough for two pies each), defrosted and allowed to rise, as per package directions

1 (3 ounce) jar anchovies packed in olive oil, drained

1 cup oil-cured black olives, pitted and cut in half

FOR THE SALAD:

8 cups assorted baby salad greens

6 tablespoons extra-virgin olive oil

2 tablespoons freshly squeezed lemon juice

Sea salt

1. Prepare the onions: Put the onions, olive oil, butter, kosher salt, a few grindings of pepper, and the bunch of thyme into a medium-size saucepan. Heat over medium-low heat until the butter melts and the onions begin to collapse, about 5 minutes, then reduce the heat to low and cook, stirring once in a while, until the onions are soft and golden, about 40 minutes.

2. Fish out the denuded twigs of thyme, and toss them. Set the onions aside at room temperature until you need them.

3. Preheat the oven to 375°F. Have several cookie sheets on hand.

4. Time to play with the dough. Cut each round of dough into fourths, then roll each quarter into a ball. Then, pulling and coaxing, flatten the dough balls into

THE TWO OF US . . . AND FRIENDS

6-inch rounds, leaving the edges thicker than the middle. Pinch closed any holes that form (oh, and they will form). Arrange the rounds on cookie sheets as you make them.

5. The tarts are assembled as follows: Divide the onions among the sixteen tarts, being as generous as you can. Pat the onions down into the pizza dough, then decorate the top of each pissaliadere with an anchovy and a few olive halves—make a smiley face! Make a division sign! Go crazy!—and pop the cookie sheets into the oven. You can bake these in stages, depending on the size of your oven and the number of cookie sheets you own.

6. Bake for 25 to 30 minutes, until the edges are golden and you see some further browning of the onions. Remove the tarts from the oven and let them cool on the baking sheets until they're at room temperature. (If you make these the day before the party, wrap them in plastic wrap once they have cooled, and chill. To serve, allow them to return to room temperature while you make the salad.)

7. To serve, toss the salad greens with the olive oil, lemon juice, and a pinch of sea salt. Each tart should be cut into quarters, and topped with a small handful of salad, almost as a garnish. Once the salad is in play, serve the pissaladieres immediately.

TIME: *Less than 2 hours total, about 30 minutes of working time*
FEEDS: *Makes 16 single-serving pissaladieres*

Place-Saving Napkin Rings

THIS IS A clever way to personalize a table, for pennies. To get the ribbon, try eBay or mandjtrimmings.com; the rubber stamps are also easily found at craft and stationery stores.

ARTISTIC TALENT LEVEL: LOW

YOU WILL NEED:

6 yards of 2-inch grosgrain ribbon, in a light or bright color

Scissors

Ruler

A rubber stamp set of the alphabet

A permanent ink inkpad, in a complementary color to the ribbon

USE WATERPROOF STAMP INK IN CASE THE RIBBON GETS WET IN A SPILL

YOU CAN RE-USE THE RIBBON TO WRAP SMALL PRESENTS

1. Snip the ribbon into foot-long lengths, giving it a bit of flair by making the cut on the diagonal. You'll have extras, but hey, you might make a mistake. Make a sample knot around a napkin, then slide it off, keeping the ribbon knotted. Repeat with the other lengths of ribbon.

2. Referencing your guest list, start marking up the loose ends of the napkin rings with the guests' initials, or their nicknames, or their first names: "Sparky" or "JFK" or "Candace." Give the ink a few moments to set, then you can slide your ribbon knots around napkins, and set them around the table at the appropriate places.

Garlicky Leg of Lamb

*L*EG OF LAMB, like roast chicken, is a dinner party fundamental. Some people shy away from it because it seems a challenge to carve, but see my little drawing (page 208) for a few hints. In fact, once you try it, you'll see it's easier than chicken for a crowd like this: where two legs of lamb will do, you'd need six or eight chickens!

Lamb positively acts like a sponge with flavors, more so than any other meat, in my thoroughly unscientific opinion. And there's nothing better with lamb than garlic. The yogurt adds a tang and tenderizes the meat as well.

2 cups plain Greek yogurt

2 teaspoons cayenne pepper

2 large sprigs rosemary, stemmed and chopped

20 cloves garlic, crushed and chopped

4 teaspoons kosher salt

4 whole heads garlic

2 legs of lamb, aitchbone removed

1. Early in the day, combine the yogurt, cayenne pepper, rosemary, garlic, and the kosher salt in a small bowl. Slather the marinade all over the legs of lamb, which should be covered and left to marinate for at least 4 hours. Take the lamb out of the refrigerator at least 30 minutes before you plan to roast it.

2. Preheat the oven to 400°F.

3. Place the roasting racks in the middle of a very large roasting pan (or two smaller ones). Heave the lamb onto the racks. Wipe off any excess yogurt. Cover any exposed bone with a piece of foil. Cut the crowns off the four heads of garlic, and toss the garlic into the bottom of the roasting pan. Add 1 cup of water.

4. Reduce the temperature to 375°F, and roast for 1¼ to 1½ hours. The lamb is done when a meat thermometer inserted into the thickest part reads 135°F for medium-rare. Make sure you factor in plenty of time to let the lamb sit when it's out of the oven—at least 30 minutes, and it can be much longer. Letting it sit is essential because it allows the juices to redistribute throughout the lamb. I actually like the lamb warm, not hot; I think the flavors show to their best advantage that way. Another great thing about leg of lamb is that you get all sorts of done-

ness levels—ranging from medium rare to medium well, for those people who have preferences. Serve the roasted garlic cloves alongside the lamb.

TIME: *Plan on half a day for marinating, roasting, and resting—you can even have the lamb out of the oven by the time the guests come and serve it warm or at room temperature. It's equally delicious, and easier to manage.*
FEEDS: *16, lavishly*
SPECIAL EQUIPMENT: *2 good, sturdy roasting racks are essential*

Carving Leg of Lamb

Two things you need to carve a leg of lamb properly: a sharp knife and a firm grip. Here's the general idea:

First, holding the lamb at a 45-degree angle, slice the round end of the lamb perpendicularly to the bone until you can slice no more.

Then, roll the leg over, and repeat with the underside. The top of the leg—really the shank—should be sliced thinly, working parallel to the bone.

Arrange the meat on a platter, add a bit of garnish in the form of the roasted garlic and some sprigs of rosemary, and it's ready for the ravening hoards.

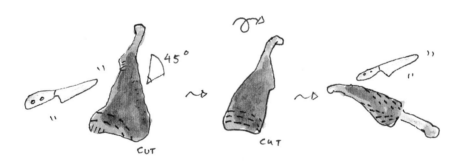

CUT   CUT

Spicy Indian Cauliflower

*W*E RECENTLY WENT out to dinner with our friends Isabelle and Ronny, to a fairly posh Indian-inspired restaurant. The cauliflower, both sweet and spicy, was dangerously addictive. Just think: "cauliflower" and "dangerously addictive" together in the same sentence! So this is my mock-up of that cauliflower, probably not terribly faithful, but still good. And this is officially the only recipe in the book where I call for Heinz ketchup.

3 tablespoons vegetable oil

3/4 cup ketchup (Heinz really is the best)

1/4 cup brown sugar

2 tablespoons light molasses

1 1/2 teaspoons ground cumin

1 teaspoon salt

1/4 teaspoon cayenne pepper

1 1/2 teaspoons paprika

2 heads cauliflower, trimmed and sectioned into large florets

1/2 cup chicken stock or water

1. Preheat the oven to 400°F. Prepare a shallow roasting pan or rimmed baking sheet by lining it with parchment paper, then greasing the paper with the vegetable oil.

2. In the bottom of a large mixing bowl, combine the ketchup, sugar, molasses, cumin, salt, cayenne, and paprika, and give it a good swirl with a spoon or your index finger. Add the prepped cauliflower, and toss the veggies carefully in the sauce, getting it in every nook and cranny.

3. Tumble the cauliflower onto the parchment paper, arranging it in a single layer. Pour the bit of chicken stock around the edges, and slide the pan into the oven.

4. Bake the cauliflower for 40 to 45 minutes, until the florets turn a deep, shellacked red. Serve hot.

TIME: *Less than an hour, mostly oven time*
FEEDS: *16, as a side dish*

Couscous with Herbs

O COUSCOUS, THE host and hostess's best friend! Couscous, cheap as can be! Couscous, done in minutes! O Couscous, how we love thee!

4 cups couscous

3½ cups chicken stock, boiling

¼ cup snipped fresh chives

¼ cup chopped fresh parsley

2 tablespoons chopped mint

4 tablespoons (½ stick) unsalted butter, softened

1½ teaspoons kosher salt

1. Pour the couscous into a medium-size mixing bowl, and add the chicken stock. Cover the bowl tightly with plastic wrap, and let the couscous sit until the stock has been absorbed, about 15 minutes.
2. Uncover, and fluff with a fork. Mix in the herbs, softened butter, and salt. Taste and correct for seasoning, and serve immediately.

TIME: *Less than 20 minutes, almost entirely unattended*
FEEDS: *Makes enough for 16 as a generous side dish*

A NOTE ON WINE

*A*RE YOU CONFUSED about wine? Not snooty enough to know the difference between a Shiraz and a Pinot Noir? Never fear. Just talk to your local wine merchant. He'll know something about his wares, and if you tell him what you're having, he can recommend something that won't break the bank. If you're still unsure, there are now some great online wine sources with very individual and charming points of view, including gratefulpalate.com in California (also a great source for bacon), and my local guy, Jeff Hoch, at winesby.com.

The Basics
Building a Buffet

This dinner, while a lot of cooking beforehand, should be a relative snap to serve. The first course should be at everyone's place when your friends first sit down, then, after a small break, the platters full of lamb, cauliflower, and couscous should come rolling out.

If possible, set up the buffet as close to the table as you can—this way, people return to the table rather than losing their way and having a fifteen-minute conversation in the kitchen or hallway. And despite the temptation to busy up your sideboard with lots of herb fronds and crystal bowls filled with who-knows-what, simple, pretty platters and big serving spoons are your best bet. The less complicated it is to get to the food, the better for you and your friends.

The cake can be served at the table, cutting pieces to appetites as people like. This should absolutely be the most relaxed part of the evening.

And one more note: Any wines should be opened before people get there—it's fun at smaller dinner parties to open bottle by bottle, but it's much easier if the bottles are ready to go when they're needed.

Deepest, Darkest Chocolate Spice Cake

*J*S IS RATHER antichocolate—he is (disgustingly) the sort of person who would prefer carrot sticks to chocolate cake. However, an informal telephone poll of ten girls revealed that they all like chocolate, and that eight out of ten think JS is insane. So here's an easy chocolate cake that tastes better the day (or even two days) after it is made. Perfect for your impossible dinner party dream!

10 ounces good-quality bittersweet or semi-sweet chocolate

10 ounces blanched almonds

1 teaspoon ground allspice

1 teaspoon ground ginger

1/2 teaspoon ground cloves

1/2 pound (2 sticks) butter, softened

2/3 cup sugar

5 eggs, separated, at room temperature

1/2 teaspoon pure vanilla extract

Pinch of cream of tartar

1. Preheat the oven to 325°F. Butter the bottom of a 9-inch springform pan, line the bottom of the pan with parchment paper, then butter the paper.

2. Set up a double boiler, making sure the water in the bottom is hot but not boiling. Break up the chocolate bars, and add them to the top of the double boiler, letting them melt. Stir the chocolate with a rubber spatula until smooth. Remove from the heat and set aside to cool.

3. Throw the blanched almonds in your food processor, whiz until very fine, then decant into a mixing bowl. You will have about 2½ cups of ground almonds. Add the allspice, ginger, and ground cloves, and mix to combine.

4. In the bowl of your mixer, whip the butter until it is smooth, then add the sugar and mix until fluffy. Add the egg yolks and give the mixture a good turn until there are no streaks of yolk remaining. Mix in the cooled chocolate, then add the spiced almond mixture. Take the bowl out of the mixer, and give the beaters a good wash and a thorough dry.

5. Pour the egg whites into a new, very clean bowl. Start beating on low, to break up the albumen, then add the pinch of cream of tartar and speed the mixer up, beating the egg whites until they are stiff but still shiny.

6. The chocolate batter will be very stiff, so lighten it by whisking in a quarter of the egg whites. When it has been loosened up a bit, gently fold in the remaining egg whites, not bothering to perfectly combine the two—a streak or two is perfectly fine—or else the egg whites will totally collapse. Pour the batter into the prepared pan, and smooth the top of the cake.

7. Bake for 40 to 45 minutes. Enjoy the best of all kitchen smells, a baking chocolate cake. But the biggest sin would be to overbake this cake—you want it rich and moist. If you test it with a toothpick, expect to see a few crumbs sticking to the wood, but it shouldn't be runny. Let the cake sit on a cooling rack in its pan until it cools, then run a knife around the edges, and unlock and remove the springform sides. You can sprinkle the top with confectioners' sugar, and serve with Real Whipped Cream (page 214).

TIME: *An hour, give or take a few minutes*

FEEDS: *16*

SPECIAL EQUIPMENT: *A standing mixer is very helpful here, but your average hand mixer will work admirably, too. And for the almonds, a food processor or blender makes life much easier. A double boiler is easily faked by resting a stainless-steel bowl or small saucepan in a skillet full of simmering water.*

Real Whipped Cream

*I*N GERMAN, *SCHLAG.* In French, *crème Chantilly.* No matter what language, the real thing is by far the best, and perfect for this dessert. Here's a trick that you should know: put the bowl of your mixer in the freezer, and the cream will whip faster.

3 cups heavy whipping cream   ¼ teaspoon pure vanilla extract
⅔ cup sifted confectioners' sugar

1. Hours before you want the whipped cream, put the bowl of a mixer or another metal mixing bowl in the freezer.
2. To prepare, pour the whipping cream into the chilled bowl, and beat the cream at medium speed until soft peaks form. You want billowy, luscious, soft mounds. Be careful about overbeating, though, because that gives you . . . butter.
3. Sift the confectioners' sugar over the top of the whipping cream, then gently fold it, along with the drop of vanilla extract, into the whipped cream. Mound in a bowl and it's ready to serve.

TIME: *A few minutes, but remember to freeze the mixing bowl!*
FEEDS: *Makes enough for 16 dollops*

SMALL TERRA-COTTA pots filled with posies marching up and down a table. It looks very professional but only requires a trip to the local florist, which sells not only small flats of ivy or posies, but the pots to put them in. When you replant the flowers, make sure to water them well. You can also buy a bit of Spanish moss to tuck around the base of the flowers, hiding the soil. Just be careful! One year, my mother set a pot of flowers on fire by placing the Spanish moss just a wee bit too close to a candle. Char is not a look we're going for here.

POTTED FLOWER

Cocktails on the Cheap for 24

Anybody with a brain and the means to do so gets the heck out of New York City on August weekends, but JS and I, apparently, have neither. Nor do our friends Jordan and Pierre, who live in Queens and have an apartment perfect for throwing parties, which in New York translates into an apartment with standing room for more than six. So we concocted a plan to have a cocktail party. Lo and behold, many of our friends had no place to go and nothing to do on August weekends, either.

But there was a major caveat: we wanted to do the whole thing, booze and all, for under $240, or about ten bucks a person. (In fact, I think I still owe Jordan $20). Also, we only had one day to cook, clean, and set up. Division of labor was key: Jordan was in charge of the drinks and the decor, while I was the girl at the stove. With the air conditioner cranked to eleven, and many bottles of Prosecco chilling in the sink, we had quite a successful summer cocktail party, and we could still afford to go to the movies the next day.

Party-Planning Time Line

TWO DAYS BEFORE:

BE HOUSE PROUD: Along with doing a good cleaning, make some party decorations, like party bunting (see page 236) and customized napkins (see page 225).
AT THE BAR: Stock up on reasonably priced beer and wine; include a limited choice of sodas, seltzer, and fruit juice.

ONE DAY BEFORE:

BE HOUSE PROUD: Make sure you have enough glasses and cups for the soup; buy and arrange flowers.
AT THE BAR: Buy ice, and set up the bar area.
IN THE KITCHEN: Make and refrigerate the avgolemono soup; prep the veggies and dressing for the crudités; roast the eggplant for the fritters; and make the shallots and polenta wedges.

DAY OF:

BE HOUSE PROUD: Hang your bunting and set up a table to use as a buffet.
IN THE KITCHEN: With the help of a friend, make the remainder of the recipes, keeping things wrapped in plastic at room temperature. The only caveats? Don't assemble the BLTs, and keep the crème fraîche for the chickpea fritters and the green goddess dressing refrigerated until party time.

RIGHT BEFORE:

BE HOUSE PROUD: Set the scene with some good party music and soft light.
AT THE BAR: Set out the chilled drinks, keeping the beer and the white wine in buckets of ice for easy self-serve.
IN THE KITCHEN: With a bit of help, set up platters of food and pour the soup into little cups. During the party, keep an eye out and replenish as necessary.

Eggplant Fritters

*T*HESE DON'T HAVE a very pronounced eggplant taste—just a creaminess complemented nicely by the crunch of the fried crust.

1 large eggplant (about 2½ pounds)

4 cloves garlic, 2 slivered, 2 grated

1 tablespoon olive oil

1 tablespoon Dijon mustard

½ cup dried bread crumbs, plus extra

½ cup chopped fresh parsley, plus extra
   for garnish

⅔ cup freshly grated Parmesan cheese

1½ teaspoons kosher salt

Pepper

1 egg

¾ cup all-purpose flour

Vegetable oil, for frying

Coarse sea salt, for serving

1. Preheat your oven to 300°F. Wash and dry the eggplant, then pierce it all over with a sharp paring knife. Insert slivers of garlic into the little incisions and rub the eggplant all over with the olive oil. Place on a rimmed cookie sheet and bake for an hour, or until the eggplant deflates like a balloon.

2. Pull the eggplant out of the oven and let cool, then pull off the skin with your fingers. Chop the cooked eggplant, putting the pulp in a fine-mesh sieve, and let it drain in the sink for 15 minutes. Turn it out into a mixing bowl, along with the grated garlic cloves, Dijon mustard, dried breadcrumbs, parsley, Parmesan, and kosher salt and pepper. Give the mixture a taste, before you add the egg— it might need more salt for your taste. If it's still very wet, add more bread crumbs as you see fit—you need to be able to make little cakes for frying. Add the egg, and mix to combine.

3. Pour vegetable oil ¼-inch deep in a deep-sided skillet, and heat over medium-high heat for a minute. Meanwhile, put the flour on a dinner plate, scoop up heaping tablespoons of the eggplant mixture, and form them into little oval patties. Dredge the patties in the flour, and then slip them into the hot oil, frying them until golden brown on both sides, about 3 minutes a side. Regulate the heat

so they don't burn. Transfer the finished patties to a paper towel–lined tray until you need them.

4. To serve, arrange the patties on a platter and sprinkle them with parsley and coarse sea salt.

TIME: *30 minutes active time; give yourself enough time to roast the egg-plant, which can be done the day before*
FEEDS: *Makes about 35 fritters*

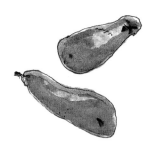

Chickpea Fritters
with Yogurt-Cumin Sauce

*T*HESE ARE A bit spicy, a bit crumbly, and topped with a creamy sauce. They're borderline addictive, and can be made into larger patties as a side dish for grilled chicken.

FOR THE FRITTERS:

1 (20-ounce) can chickpeas, drained and rinsed

¼ teaspoon cayenne pepper

½ teaspoon ground cumin

½ cup chopped fresh parsley

1 teaspoon kosher salt

1 egg

⅔ cup bread crumbs

Vegetable oil, for frying

FOR THE SAUCE:

1 cup Greek yogurt

Zest and juice of ½ lemon

1 teaspoon ground cumin

½ teaspoon sea salt

1. Set up a deep-sided skillet on the stove, and fill it ¼-inch deep with vegetable oil.
2. Tumble the chickpeas into a mixing bowl, and mash them with a fork, pulverizing some and leaving others mostly whole. Add the cayenne pepper, cumin, parsley, salt, and egg, and mix to combine. Turn the heat on under the skillet, and pour the bread crumbs on a dinner plate.
3. Form heaping tablespoons of the mixture into balls, then roll them in the bread crumbs. Slip them into the hot fat, turning carefully (using two forks to maneuver them can be helpful) until browned all over, about 5 minutes. One or two will fall apart—just fish the remains out of the skillet so they don't burn, and give yourself a cook's treat. Drain the finished chickpea fritters on paper towels until needed.
4. Make the sauce: Mix the yogurt, lemon juice and zest, cumin, and sea salt in a small bowl (or even the yogurt container) until combined, and refrigerate until needed.

5. To serve, dot the tops of the now room-temperature fritters with the yogurt sauce and arrange on a platter.

TIME: *About 30 minutes*
FEEDS: *Makes about 35 fritters*

Organizing a Cocktail Party

Here's a secret: when the food is gone, the guests are gone, too. So when you plan a cocktail party, don't plan on feeding people for hours on end. Just three hours on end. And let them know that—by not starting your party at nine at night, when they'll expect dinner and then hang out for the rest of the evening, but at five thirty, when they'll understand that dinner is not involved. Providing dinner makes for a more expensive party, but if the time is finite, and the food is, too, you will get just as much party as you want to pay for.

The math is as follows: three to five pieces of food per person, per hour; so for this party, you want somewhere south of 360 tidbits. And that's it. No ordering pizza. No panicking that there's not enough. There will be plenty—after all, this is cocktails, and everybody will be going out to dinner afterward, anyway.

Organizing the room is also important. Don't put the bar near the front door or near the kitchen—if it's near the front door, people never move into your house, and if it's in the kitchen, you'll never get people out of the kitchen so they can admire your homemade party bunting. Scatter the food around—two or three stations are nice—so there's natural circulation as people graze and taste the hors d'oeuvres.

Finally, all these bites (save the soup) are designed to be eaten in one pop, so there's no need to deal with plates or utensils. Glasses and napkins are all that you require.

Invitations and RSVPs

For this party, we mailed out postcards with photographs of 1950s children playing stickball in Brooklyn. We were in Queens, but you get the point. I think people take paper invitations more seriously than e-mailed ones. When it comes to RSVPs, do give out your e-mail address as well as your telephone number. E-mail lends itself to RSVPing, since you don't have to leave an awkward message on somebody's voice mail. Of course, we don't live in an RSVP generation. I recently went to a wedding where not one of JS's friends had bothered to RSVP, but of course they all showed up (the siren call of free beer is irresistible). Some gentle prodding will always be necessary, but don't feel you're being pushy. You need to have a ballpark idea of how many people to expect, and it's only polite that people let you know if they can come.

Mini BLTs

*T*HESE ARE ALWAYS a huge hit. There's something about the cholesterol-fest that is mayo and bacon that makes these hors d'oeuvres irresistible.

½ cup prepared mayonnaise

1 tablespoon Dijon mustard

Squeeze of fresh lemon juice

1 clove garlic

1 baguette

1 large bunch of basil, washed, dried, and leaves separated

5 slices bacon

1 pint cherry or grape tomatoes, cut in half (yellow ones are particularly cute here)

1. Make the mayonnaise: Mix the mayo with the Dijon and the lemon juice, then grate the garlic clove over the top and mix. Refrigerate until needed.
2. Preheat the oven to 350°F.
3. Slice the baguette very thinly—less than a ¼-inch thick—until you have forty bread rounds. Lay them out in a single layer on a cookie sheet and toast until dry and lightly golden. Stack them in a corner of your kitchen until needed.
4. Cook the bacon. Some people like to do it in the microwave, but I still cook it the old-fashioned way: in a skillet, over very low heat. You want very crispy bacon here, about 8 minutes cooking time, turning several times. Drain on paper towels, and crumble it well.
5. Assemble. A second pair of hands is useful here: Take a round of toast and give it a dab of mayo, which acts like very tasty glue. Top with a small basil leaf, a pinch of crumbled bacon, and half a grape tomato. Line them up on a cutting board or platter and watch them disappear.

TIME: *With a bit of organization, 10 minutes*
FEEDS: *Makes 40 BLTs*

Stamped Napkins

PAPER NAPKINS ARE an evil necessity, but since they're used once and thrown away, I guess there's no need to lose sleep over them. Except I do. And then I come up with a solution to make the napkins less boring, so that, before you wipe your face with one, you think, "Gee, isn't this napkin cute!"

ARTISTIC TALENT METER: LOW

YOU WILL NEED:

2 (30-count) packages white cocktail napkins

Rubber stamps: letters, numbers, little icons—your choice

Several colors of waterproof ink pads

Use the napkins to channel your creative vision—whether it's a wineglass, your initials, the word "party," a bunch of stars—by stamping them using the waterproof ink pads. They can all be the same, they can all be different; it is up to you! For a party of 24, make 48.

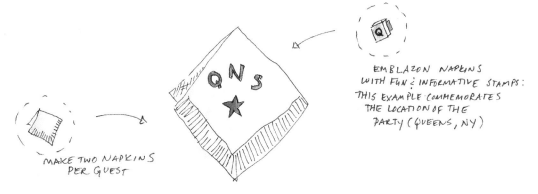

MAKE TWO NAPKINS PER GUEST

EMBLAZON NAPKINS WITH FUN & INFORMATIVE STAMPS: THIS EXAMPLE COMMEMORATES THE LOCATION OF THE PARTY (QUEENS, NY)

Frittata with Mushrooms and Green Beans

HERE'S A BIT of protein in the middle of all these vegetables. There's a reason for that. Protein is expensive. Vegetables and grains are cheap. But eggs are the golden mean—both cheap and protein. Eat up!

8 ounces green beans, trimmed

1 teaspoon vegetable oil

8 ounces button mushrooms, wiped clean and sliced

3 tablespoons butter

1 teaspoon chopped fresh thyme

9 eggs

1 teaspoon salt

Pepper

¼ cup finely chopped fresh parsley

Sea salt

1. This is a one-pan event. Fill a large, nonstick skillet with about an inch of water, bring it to a boil, and add the green beans. Cook for about 2 minutes, until the green beans turn electric green and they're slightly tender to the bite. Drain them and run the beans under cold water to stop the cooking. Set aside.

2. Heat the drizzle of oil in the same nonstick pan for a minute over high heat, then add the mushrooms, shaking the pan and stirring as the mushrooms sizzle away. After another minute, add 2 tablespoons of the butter on the top. Shake often, allowing the butter to make its way down to the bottom of the pan. Add the thyme. After 5 minutes, the mushrooms should be developing wonderful color and fragrance, and the butter should be melted.

3. Crack the eggs into a mixing bowl, add ¼ cup water, and beat lightly with a fork, adding the salt and freshly ground pepper at the end. Right before you're ready to pour in the eggs, toss the last pat of butter, the beans, and the chopped parsley into the pan with the mushrooms, then arrange the veggies so that there's an even layer in the bottom of the pan. Pour the egg over the top, tilting the pan so every corner gets its share.

4. Cook over low heat, covered, for 12 to 15 minutes, checking occasionally. The frittata will be done when there's no liquid egg and the top has puffed up, soufflé style. Flip the omelet out onto a cutting board and let it cool.

5. To serve, cut it into little bite-size squares, about 1½ inches long, and give each top a tiny sprinkle of good salt. Arrange on a platter and let the hordes feed.

TIME: *About 30 minutes, but this can be made ahead (even the day before) and served at room temperature*
FEEDS: *Makes about 48 little squares*
SPECIAL EQUIPMENT: *A nonstick pan makes your frittata-ing much easier*

Polenta Triangles with Ricotta and Caramelized Onions

*T*HIS DISH IS particularly good with real polenta, meaning not instant, and that's the way I wrote the recipe. But you can make instant polenta according to the directions and serve it the same way.

2 tablespoons butter

5 large red onions, sliced into half-moons

1 tablespoon brown sugar

1 teaspoon kosher salt

1½ cups polenta, preferably not the instant variety

5 cups canned chicken stock

1 large sprig rosemary

1 cup whole-milk ricotta cheese

Pinch of freshly grated nutmeg

1. Begin to melt the butter in a deep-sided saucepan over medium heat, and add the onions, shaking and stirring to coat all the slivers. Cook for a few minutes, until the onions begin to collapse, then add the brown sugar and kosher salt, stirring to combine. Cook over low heat, stirring from time to time, for about 40 minutes, until the onions are deeply browned and velvety.

2. Prep a cookie sheet or cutting board by spraying it with a light coating of non-stick spray.

3. Bring 5 cups of chicken stock and the sprig of rosemary to a rapid boil in a medium-size saucepan, and then add the polenta in a steady, slow stream, stirring continuously to fight the good fight against lumps. (If you're using instant polenta, follow the instructions on the package for making six portions.) Stir continuously for 1 minute, then cover the pan and cook over low heat for 10 minutes. Repeat the 1-minute-and-10-minute routine twice more, until the polenta is fully cooked. Remove and toss out the now tragic-looking rosemary sprig and pour the polenta out on the prepped cookie sheet, smoothing out until

you have a vaguely rectangular blob of polenta about ½ inch thick. Let it cool completely.

4. Mix the ricotta with the nutmeg. Then, to serve, cut the polenta into little triangles, about 1 inch per side. Top each with ¼ teaspoonful of the ricotta and a small helping of the caramelized onions. Arrange on a platter, and you're good to go.

TIME: *About an hour, cooking time, and 15 minutes party prep time*
FEEDS: *Makes about 40 polenta triangles*

Party Supplies on the Cheap

My favorite locale for cheap party items is the famous Pearl River department store, on Broadway, near Chinatown. Pearl River's irresistible tchochkes are available on their Web site, pearlriver.com. Go ahead, gorge yourself on chopsticks, dollar tea bowls, tea towels that say "Good Morning," and Chinese lanterns. This is a place to get little Chinese soup spoons or bowls to serve the avgolemono in. Another terrific source for cheap and fun party supplies is the Tesoros Trading Company, tesoros.com. This site has great Mexican oilcloth tablecloths, but I like it the best around Christmastime, where I always buy several strange Peruvian charms to use as tree ornaments.

Potato-Herb Bites

POTATO. HERBS. CHEESE. It's no surprise that these are a crowd favorite.

2 tablespoons snipped fresh chives	1 clove garlic, grated
1 tablespoon chopped fresh mint	1 cup fresh goat cheese
1 tablespoon chopped fresh tarragon	Sea salt and pepper
2 tablespoons chopped fresh basil	3 pounds fingerling potatoes

1. Make the cheese topping: Mix the herbs with the garlic and goat cheese in a small bowl, and mix to combine. Taste and correct for salt. Refrigerate until needed.
2. Scrub the fingerlings, then put them in a large saucepan filled with cold water. Bring them to a boil, and cook until just tender when pierced with a paring knife, 15 to 18 minutes (the cooking time will depend on the freshness of your potatoes, so keep a watchful eye). Drain the potatoes and run them under a cold tap.
3. To serve, slice the now room-temperature potatoes into inch-thick rounds, and arrange them like coins on a platter. Top each round with a dab of the herbed cheese mixture.

TIME: *20 minutes cooking time, 10 minutes assembly time*
FEEDS: *Makes about 50 potato rounds*
SPECIAL EQUIPMENT: *Jordan has one of those mini food processors that made whizzing the herbs extremely easy. But doing it by hand is not a big time drain.*

Zucchini Rounds with Parmesan

*T*HIS HORS D'OEUVRE IS modeled after a simple summer salad. It has pleasing textures—the softness of the grilled zukes, the crunchiness of the almonds, the crystalline pop of the Parmesan. A happy little bite for a party.

4 medium zucchini

3 tablespoons olive oil

Hunk of Parmesan (at least 6 ounces)

½ cup chopped smoked almonds

1. Soak the zucchini in a bowl of cold water for 10 minutes, then rinse and dry. Slice on the diagonal into ovals about ½ inch thick. Toss in a salad bowl with the olive oil.
2. Heat a grill pan over high heat. Grill the zucchini rounds in batches, about 2 minutes a side, so you get nice grill marks on both sides. Transfer the finished zuke slices onto a platter to cool.
3. To serve, whip out your trusty vegetable peeler and shave curls of Parmesan off the hunk of cheese. Put a curl on top of each zucchini oval, and top that with a pinch of the chopped almonds.

TIME: *About 15 minutes cooking time, and 10 minutes setup time*
FEEDS: *Makes about 48 rounds*
SPECIAL EQUIPMENT: *A stovetop grill or grill pan*

Avgolemono Soup with Mint

$\mathcal{T}$HIS IS A traditional Greek soup, thickened with pureed rice and flavored with egg and lots of lemon. It works perfectly for a party soup shot.

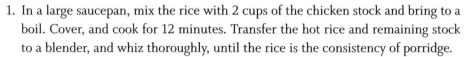

8 cups chicken stock	Juice of 3 lemons
2/3 cup basmati rice	Zest of 1/2 a lemon
1 tablespoon salt	1/3 cup finely chopped mint
3 eggs, plus 3 egg yolks	1/2 cup finely diced hothouse cucumber

1. In a large saucepan, mix the rice with 2 cups of the chicken stock and bring to a boil. Cover, and cook for 12 minutes. Transfer the hot rice and remaining stock to a blender, and whiz thoroughly, until the rice is the consistency of porridge.
2. Pour the remaining stock in the same pot, add the pureed rice, and bring to a gentle boil. Add the salt, and reduce the heat to a bare simmer.
3. Beat the egg and egg yolks lightly in a mixing bowl, then add a ladleful of the soup, whisking the soup and eggs together. This mixture goes back into the soup pot and gets swirled about. Turn off the heat, and add the lemon juice and lemon zest. Taste for salt, then let cool and refrigerate.
4. To serve, ladle 1/3-cup servings into tea cups or little soup cups (see page 230). Drop a few tiny cubes of cucumber and a pinch of mint on the top.

TIME: *About 20 minutes cooking time, but several hours to cool*
FEEDS: *24 small servings, or enough for 6 as a first course*
SPECIAL EQUIPMENT: *That blender is for more than just daquiris. I'm just saying.*

All-Green Crudités with Green Goddess Dip

CRUDITÉS ARE USUALLY the ugly sister at cocktail parties—a cabbage head hollowed out and filled with ranch dressing, and several emaciated carrots piled around it. But if you make crudités pretty—in this case, arranging vegetables that range from pale chartreuse to bright grass green—people will be drawn to them. The dip is a riff on a very old-fashioned salad dressing, cool, creamy, and herby.

FOR THE GREEN GODDESS DIP:

1 anchovy

Juice and zest of 1 lemon

3/4 cup sour cream

1/2 cup mayonnaise

3 tablespoons finely chopped fresh tarragon

3 tablespoons finely snipped fresh chives

Sea salt and pepper

FOR THE CRUDITÉS:

12 ounces green beans, trimmed

2 bunches of asparagus, trimmed and ends peeled

1 teaspoon kosher salt

2 bulbs fennel, washed

1 head romaine lettuce, outer leaves discarded

2 hothouse cucumbers, peeled, halved lengthwise, and seeded

1. Muddle the anchovy in the lemon juice and zest in the bottom of a small bowl. Add the sour cream and mayonnaise, and mix well. Fold in the herbs, and then add salt and pepper to taste. Refrigerate until needed.

2. For the crudités: The green beans and the asparagus need to be blanched. Heat 2 inches of water in a deep-sided skillet, add the salt when it comes to a boil, then add the green beans. Cook for 2 minutes, until the beans become bright and give a little when bitten into. Rescue them from the hot water with tongs or a bamboo-handled strainer, and run them under cold water to stop the cooking. Cook the asparagus using the same boiling water, boiling the asparagus for 3 to 4 minutes, until tender-firm. Repeat cold water trick to stop cooking.

3. The fennel branches should not be trimmed too radically, because they'll be useful as dipping handles: just core and cut the fennel lengthwise, separating the

pieces as you do. The romaine leaves can be left alone, the smaller the better. Cut the cucumbers on the diagonal into long Us.

4. To serve, arrange the vegetables attractively on a plate around the bowl of green goddess dressing.

TIME: *About 30 minutes, including all the asparagus peeling*
FEEDS: *Makes enough for a 24-person party, of course*

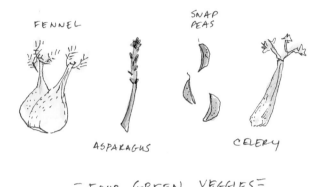

FENNEL

SNAP PEAS

ASPARAGUS

CELERY

= FOUR GREEN VEGGIES =

WHAT ABOUT BOOZE?
CURING YOUR (EXPENSIVE) DRINKING PROBLEM

*Y*OU'D BE SURPRISED to learn how much wine under $10 you can buy out there that isn't in a box or from that utopia known as Boone's Farm. In fact, you should be able to buy a case of completely decent wine (enough for this party) for less than $100, leaving you some playing room for beer, and maybe a bit of (not top-shelf) hard alcohol that you can make into a mixed drink—Mojitos still being very popular, and very refreshing.

Party Bunting

COMPLETELY FRIVOLOUS, BUT having a party is completely frivolous, too. This involves stringing together bits of fabric remnants on a piece of rickrack, and then winding it around your banister or tacking it to your wall. Silly, but very charming. You can find remnants—the odds and ends of fabric bolts—at any fabric store, such as Jo-Ann Fabrics.

ARTISTIC TALENT METER: MEDIUM

YOU WILL NEED:

Several yards of remnant fabrics, preferably cotton, in several different patterns and colors
6 yards of ½-inch rickrack in a bright color
Pinking shears
Scissors
Straight pins
Thread that matches the rickrack
A sewing machine

1. Iron the fabrics that you've collected, then cut out little flags using your pinking shears. Make them about 8 × 8 × 4 inches, but don't bother to measure them. They should be free-form. You will need about 36 little flags.

2. Using the straight pins, pin the flags by the short side to the rickrack, starting about one yard into the rickrack, to give yourself a way to tie the rickrack to your staircase, bookshelf, etc. Stop pinning on flags when you have about a yard of rickrack to go.

3. Sit down at your sewing machine, and, sewing on the wrong side, use a straight stitch to attach the flags to the rickrack. That's it! Party bunting, for a bit of fun.

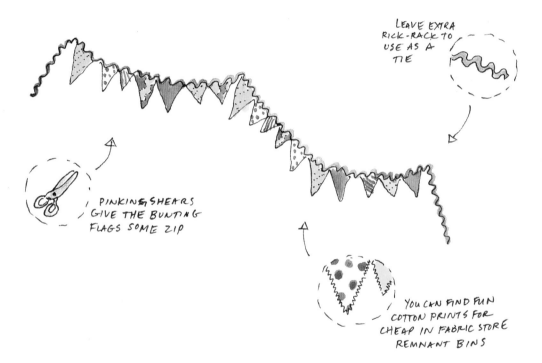

LEAVE EXTRA RICK-RACK TO USE AS A TIE

PINKING SHEARS GIVE THE BUNTING FLAGS SOME ZIP

YOU CAN FIND FUN COTTON PRINTS FOR CHEAP IN FABRIC STORE REMNANT BINS

Celebration for 32

My parents have thrown many parties over the years, but none as memorable as my mother's great triumph: a surprise party for my father for his fiftieth birthday. As a disclaimer, I will say that that party, which lasted a weekend, was a bit grander in scale than this one here. But it wasn't grander in the sense of taking place at the Plaza Hotel. There were no towering cakes or party planners running about orchestrating photo opportunities. Instead, it was a pastiche of friends and family pitching in to help make Pop's birthday weekend one of the best parties ever. A friend of my mother's, Ronna, volunteered to hem over a hundred napkins. My Aunt Mels cut dozens of bow ties, to honor my father's famous sartorial choice. My cousins organized a re-lyricized version of "Everything Old Is New Again," complete with Fosse-like choreography and costumes. It was an effort of love, so although there were over a hundred people running around, it still felt intimate and personal.

Parties at home are really the best, and worth the effort. If you like, you should split the duties of this one with a friend or two—groups hosting together increase the mix of guests and make parties all the more lively, anyway. This is the sort of party you throw to celebrate an achievement, and it's the sort of party with a guest of honor. Finally, it's the sort of party that people remember for years to come.

Hazelnut Swirls

*H*AZELNUTS, WHILE NATURALLY sweet, zing you with slight nutty bitterness at the end. Traditionally, they're used in desserts, but they work extremely well in this cocktail cracker.

2 cups raw hazelnuts

1½ teaspoons sea salt

1 (16 ounce) package (2 sheets) puff pastry, thawed

¼ pound (1 stick) butter, melted

¼ cup hazelnut oil (optional)

Flour, for dusting

Coarse sea salt, for sprinkling

1. Preheat the oven to 375°F. Put the hazelnuts on a rimmed baking sheet or in a pie plate and toast them for 10 minutes, until their skins darken to a deep burgundy. Roll them off the sheet and onto an old (but clean!) dishtowel. Fold them in the towel and rub them vigorously, peeling away as much of the skin as you can (it's impossible, and not worth it, to get it all off).

2. Blitz the peeled, toasted hazelnuts in the food processor until absolutely pulverized. Add the sea salt and blitz again. Empty the food processor bowl onto a plate and set aside.

3. Lightly flour your countertop or pastry cloth, and unfold one of the puff pastry squares. Lightly roll out the pastry, increasing the size by 1 inch in length and 1 inch in width. Brush the whole surface liberally with melted butter.

4. Cover the pastry with half of the hazelnuts, and drizzle 2 tablespoons of the oil on top. Starting at one long end, roll up the dough, tucking it tightly into a spiral. Repeat with the second sheet of puff pastry, and put both in the fridge for 15 minutes.

5. Slice the logs into ⅓-inch thick slices, laying them down flat and at least 1½ inch from each other on cookie sheets. Brush the swirls with melted butter and sprinkle with sea salt. Bake for 15 minutes, until puffed and golden at the edges. Let them cool on cookie sheets. These can be kept for several days in airtight containers.

TIME: *About an hour, mostly unattended*

FEEDS: *Makes 40 swirls*

TWO DAYS BEFORE:

IN THE KITCHEN: Make hazelnut swirls and sesame twists and store in airtight containers.

DAY BEFORE:

BE HOUSE PROUD: Collect enough forks from your friends and neighbors, count salad plates for the "supper" portion, buy napkins, get out platters, organize where the bar and buffet will be (including putting out the plates, forks, and napkins), and buy and arrange any flowers (see page 253) and decorate a few votive candle holders (see page 242).

IN THE KITCHEN: Make the shallot jam, mash the potatoes for the croquetas, and bake the blondies, keeping them in airtight containers when completely cool.

AT THE BAR: Make sure all alcoholic and nonalcoholic drinks are in the house and (if need be) in the fridge. Also, buy ice.

ANY EXTRAS: Contact any staff you might have hired, or friends that are cohosting, and review who's doing what.

DAY OF:

BE HOUSE PROUD: A quick tidy and bathroom check are essential.

IN THE KITCHEN: In the morning, marinate the tuna, and make the croquetas and the deviled eggs, prep the tomato salad, and make the dressing. Store everything in the fridge. In the afternoon, grill and refrigerate the tuna, sauté the mushrooms, and toast the bread. Finally, when your helping hands arrive, make the apple and prosciutto breadsticks.

AT THE BAR: Set up the bar, minus refrigerated items.

RIGHT BEFORE:

BE HOUSE PROUD: Turn down the lights, turn on the music, and light a votive or twelve.

IN THE KITCHEN: Have your helpers start assembling hors d'oeuvre platters—all but the deviled eggs can remain at room temperature indefinitely. Arrange nicely on the table.

You can also arrange the sliced tuna and the salad, and keep them in the fridge until needed.

AT THE BAR: Ice and cold drinks should go out now.

DURING:

IN THE KITCHEN: Check the buffet table, and replenish tidbits as necessary. After an hour, dress the salad and bring the tuna and salad, along with bread, to the buffet table.

Finally, bring out the blondies and pat yourself on the back.

Decorative Votives

AT A PARTY like this, where you might use dozens of votives scattered about several rooms, it's nice to have a few with a bit of distinction mixed in with the plain glass ones. Other than the votive holders, all you need for this project are pens that can write on glass. They're available at craft shops, and come in different levels of transparency, so they look like watercolor when the flame shines through the glass.

ARTISTIC TALENT METER: MEDIUM

YOU WILL NEED:

Clear glass votives

Glass ink pens, available at craft stores and stationery stores

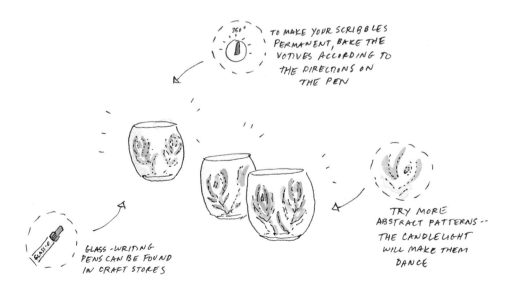

TO MAKE YOUR SCRIBBLES PERMANENT, BAKE THE VOTIVES ACCORDING TO THE DIRECTIONS ON THE PEN

GLASS-WRITING PENS CAN BE FOUND IN CRAFT STORES

TRY MORE ABSTRACT PATTERNS -- THE CANDLELIGHT WILL MAKE THEM DANCE

1. Choose a motif you like—for mine, I used feathers, but you can choose leaves, or flowers. The most important thing is that you can make an easy, sinuous line. If things get too complicated, the votives will look labored instead of pretty. Draw your design on the glass votives.

2. Be careful not to accidentally brush your fingers over your drawing before the ink has dried, or it will smudge and you'll have to be clever in masking it. (Though, in the immortal words of Bob Ross, there are no mistakes, just happy accidents.) Let the votives dry completely before using them.

The Basics
Throwing a Celebration Party

When you think about it, a party like this is odd—snacks, dinner, and dessert, and all before nine thirty. But since it's essentially a cocktail party with supper and a bite of dessert, you can't string your guests along till midnight without giving them the okay to leave. It's best to start early—around six thirty—and give your guests an end time, so they know that if they show up at eight thirty, things won't just be getting into full swing.

If you're throwing a birthday party, or an engagement party, or a party celebrating someone getting into the circus, there will be a time when people will want to stand up and embarrass your guest of honor, usually through bawdy limericks and rehashing of stories from when they were children. The perfect time to do this is between the supper course and the dessert, when your friends will be full and probably won't be agitating for more drinks.

Think about how the traffic flow will work in your house. Particularly, if you are hiring a helping hand or two (see page 251), you'll want to guide guests away from the kitchen. Guests are nosy. They want to see around your house, and they want to get a sneak peek at what's for dinner. But it's a kindness to your kitchen assistants to keep the snoopers out.

Sesame Twists

ANOTHER SAVORY TIDBIT to have laying about during early cocktail hour. These are spectacularly quick and easy to make.

2 sheets prepared piecrust dough, thawed

6 tablespoons sesame seeds

2 teaspoons coarse sea salt

3 tablespoons butter, melted

Flour, for dusting

1. Preheat the oven to 350°F.
2. Flour a pastry cloth or surface, and unroll a sheet of piecrust dough. Use your rolling pin to flatten it out a bit, then sprinkle 3 tablespoons of the sesame seeds and 1 teaspoon of the sea salt evenly over the surface. Roll the dough again, pressing the seeds into the surface of the piecrust. The finished piecrust will be quite thin.
3. Have a baking sheet at the ready, and slice the piecrust into sixteen long strips. Pick them up, give them a few twists, and lay them on the baking sheet, as close as you want. Brush the twisted strips with a bit of melted butter, and bake them in the oven until golden and crispy, 8 to 10 minutes.

TIME: *15 minutes*

FEEDS: *Makes about 32 twists*

Potato Croquetas with Smoked Trout
and Crème Fraîche

You could also call these croquettes, but that sounds like something your Aunt Gladys served on a toothpick in 1952. Instead, they're croquetas, which makes them very chic tapas.

FOR THE CROQUETAS:

2 pounds Yukon Gold potatoes

1½ tablespoons kosher salt

2 tablespoons chopped fresh dill

5 eggs

1 fillet smoked trout

½ cup all-purpose flour

2 cups panko (Japanese bread crumbs)

Vegetable oil, for frying

FOR THE SAUCE:

½ cup crème fraîche

Juice of ½ lemon

½ teaspoon sea salt

1. Put the unpeeled potatoes in a deep saucepan and cover with cold water. Add 1 tablespoon of the kosher salt, and bring the potatoes to a boil. Cook at full boil for 20 to 25 minutes, until the potatoes are very tender. Drain and let cool for 10 minutes.

2. Peel the potatoes—the skins will just pull right off—and squeeze them through a ricer into a large mixing bowl. Add the chopped dill, the remaining ½ tablespoon of kosher salt, and 3 eggs, and mix well.

3. Finely flake the fillet of smoked trout, pulling out any little bones you find.

4. Scoop out scant tablespoons of the potato, place the lump in the palm of your hand, and push your thumb into the middle to create a little dimple. Fill the dimple with a pinch of smoked trout, then roll the mashed potato into a little ball. Repeat. Repeat, repeat. I think you see where this is going.

5. When you have a small army of potato balls, set up a breading assembly line: first, a dinner plate for the flour; then, a shallow soup plate for the remaining 2 eggs beaten with 3 tablespoons of water; finally, a dinner plate for the panko. The operation is as follows: a quick roll in the flour, a dip in the egg wash, and then a good coating of the panko. Put the finished croquetas on a platter covered with waxed paper, and let them set up in the refrigerator for at least an hour.

6. Fry them: Heat at least 3 inches of vegetable oil in a heavy-bottomed saucepan to 350°F, using a frying thermometer to monitor the heat. Lower the croquetas into the hot oil, not crowding the pan, and deep-fry until golden brown, less than 5 minutes.

7. Let the croquetas cool—they can be served at room temperature. Mix the crème fraîche with the lemon juice and sea salt, and before serving the croquetas, dot the tops with the lemony crème fraîche.

TIME: *About an hour, plus unattended time*
FEEDS: *Makes 50 croquetas*
SPECIAL EQUIPMENT: *A potato ricer is essential, for the right croqueta texture; also, you need a frying (aka candy) thermometer.*

CELEBRATION DRINKS

ON A BUDGET, Prosecco is the way to go: bubbly and champagne-esque, it's decidedly more reasonably priced. I never worry about stocking hard alcohol when there's wine and beer on hand—for a party of thirty-two, you can get away with spending under $200—but if you are a gin drinker, or know that people will want a mixed drink, do so in a very limited way: only supply gin, vodka, and scotch; make sure you have tonic, club soda, orange juice, and cranberry juice; and remember to provide wedges of lemon and lime. If someone wants a margarita, they'll have to wait 'til later.

Teacup and Saucer Tiered Platter

✂

A PLATTER FOR dessert, or for cocktail hour bites. The problem with buffet tables can be lack of variation; this platter gives a bit of visual interest to the tableau. It's a great way to abuse the set of china you inherited last year from Great Aunt Zelda, or you can mix and match from odds and ends you have in the back of the cupboard. The best part? It's temporary. I'm keeping my promise about no glue guns.

ARTISTIC TALENT METER: LOW

YOU WILL NEED:

2 dinner plates, 1 salad plate, and 1 saucer

2 teacups or coffee cups

Double-sided tape

1. Obviously, this tableau needs to be set up on the buffet table itself. If you've got them, let your servers know that this is not something that can be whisked off the table.

2. Invert a dinner plate and place it face down on your table. Place several strips of double-sided tape on the base of the plate. The other dinner plate should also get the double-sided tape treatment on the bottom. Rest the other dinner plate, face up, on the first. This is the base of your platter. Invert a tea cup and place it face down in the middle of the dinner plate. Cross strips of double-sided tape on the bottom of that teacup, and balance the salad plate on top.

3. Repeat with the remaining teacup and saucer. You can use this for cocktail hour, but it's actually the perfect vehicle for the blondies.

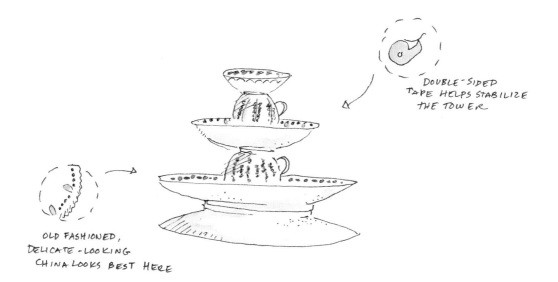

DOUBLE-SIDED TAPE HELPS STABILIZE THE TOWER

OLD FASHIONED, DELICATE-LOOKING CHINA LOOKS BEST HERE

Green Apple, Prosciutto, and Shallot Jam on a Breadstick

THESE SNACKS ARE delicious and even the most kitchen-clueless can be sat down in a corner to assemble them, once you make the shallot jam.

FOR THE SHALLOT JAM:

8 shallots, minced

2 tablespoons butter

1 tablespoon brown sugar

3 tablespoons balsamic vinegar

1 teaspoon kosher salt

FOR THE ASSEMBLY:

½ pound imported prosciutto, thinly sliced

A Granny Smith apple

25 grissini (thin Italian breadsticks), snapped in half

1. Put the shallots, butter, brown sugar, balsamic vinegar, and salt in a small saucepan, and cook, stirring occasionally, over medium-low heat for 45 minutes, until the shallots have completely given up the ghost and are just lovely caramel-colored mush. If it looks a bit dry, add 1 tablespoon of water. Set aside and let it cool at room temperature until you need the jam.

2. To assemble these snacks, first separate each slice of prosciutto into two pieces. Then core and slice the apple into julienne strips. Take a breadstick, spread about ½ teaspoon of the shallot jam on its middle, and bundle a few strips of green apple to the breadstick using the prosciutto as the twine. Ta-da!

TIME: *About an hour cooking time, and 20 minutes assembly time*
FEEDS: *Makes 50 sticks*

The Basics
Extra Help

A party this size should only be attempted if you have very devoted friends who love you and will pitch in, or with a bit of extra help from a local service. It would be ideal to have a bartender, and at least one person to help pass and replenish trays, even if you are in and out of the kitchen overseeing things.

You can always look in the Yellow Pages, but I think that college students are the way to go; often there will be a student-run service hiring out kids who know their way around a Chili's during the summertime. Another likely spot is a culinary school, if there is one nearby. These kids will certainly know the ins and outs of food protocol, and have the added advantage of knowing their way around a kitchen, so you can show them how to assemble things and they can copy it. Rates will vary with time and location, but expect to pay $35 to 50 an hour for experienced staff.

Deviled Eggs
with Asparagus and Mint

Normally, I have a firm stance against pencil-thin asparagus, and pity those who choose them over the big, fat beauties at the vegetable stand. The fatties have more flavor. However, I guess all of God's creations have their uses and I finally found one for skinny asparagus.

10 large eggs

2 tablespoons Dijon mustard

½ cup mayonnaise

Squeeze of lemon juice

1 teaspoon kosher salt, plus a pinch to salt
 the asparagus water

Pepper

2 bunches of pencil-thin asparagus

½ cup finely chopped fresh mint

1. Cover the eggs with an inch of water, and bring to a boil over high heat. Reduce the heat to medium-low so that just a few constant bubbles disturb the eggs, and boil for 10 minutes. Drain the eggs and run cool water over them.

2. When they've cooled enough to handle, crack them all over and peel them, trying not to make a hash of it. Cut the eggs in half and turn out the cooked yolks into a small bowl. Set the whites aside for now.

3. Mash the egg yolks with the back of a fork, and make a standard deviled filling by mixing in the Dijon mustard, the mayo, the squeeze of lemon to taste, 1 teaspoon of salt, and ample amounts of freshly ground pepper. Taste and correct for salt, cover, and stick into the refrigerator.

4. Heat a skillet full of water over high heat; while it's coming to a boil, break off the tough ends of the asparagus and throw them away. Add a pinch of salt to the water, then the asparagus, and cook for 2 minutes. Immediately drain them and run the asparagus under cold water to stop the cooking. When they're cool, cut all but the tips away from the asparagus. Save the tips for the party, and eat the stalks for lunch.

5. To serve, slice each egg-white half in thirds. Dot these egg-white crescents with ¼ teaspoon of the deviled yolk mixture, then rest an asparagus tip on top, along with a tiny pinch of chopped mint. Refrigerate until you need them.

TIME: *About 20 minutes prep time and 20 minutes assembly time*
FEEDS: *Makes about 60*

Flower Power
GREENS

THERE ARE MANY ways to bust your budget on a party like this, and you may want to. But this isn't your wedding. The flower budget does not need to equal the average yearly salary in a third world country. One solution is to buy out the greens selection at your local florist, or even corner market. These are cheap, because they are used as filler for bouquets, but if you can scrounge up several different colors and textures, the bouquets will be beautiful and interesting. In general, get out your largest and tallest vases—these arrangements will be statuesque. And if some of the stems are quite woody, whack them a few times with the handle of a chef's knife or a hammer, so that the water can enter the branches more easily. Finally, add a tablespoon of sugar (to feed the greens) and a squeeze of lemon juice (for clearer water) to each vase.

≡ GREENS ≡

Mushroom and Goat Cheese Toasts

*W*HO SAYS WHITE bread is passé? It makes very good little cocktail toasts. Another '60s cocktail party twist you can do with this hors d'oeuvre is to use Boursin cheese instead of the plain chèvre. It's very twee but most everybody likes Boursin.

1 loaf extra-thin white sandwich bread
  (Pepperidge Farm is a favorite variety)

1½ pounds shiitake mushrooms, stems
  removed, sliced thinly

2 tablespoons olive oil

2 cloves garlic, bruised

2 tablespoons butter

1 teaspoon sea salt

¾ cup finely chopped fresh parsley

1 (12-ounce) log fresh goat cheese, at room
  temperature

1. Preheat the oven to 325°F.
2. Prep the toasts: Lay out several pieces of white bread on your counter, whip out your rolling pin, and give them a good roll, flattening them. Cut out rounds from the flattened bread, using a 2-inch round cutter; you should get three or four per slice. Repeat this step until you have about fifty rounds.
3. Lay the rounds out on a baking sheet and toast in the oven, until very lightly golden and dried out, 12 to 15 minutes. These will burn in a moment, so keep an eagle eye on them. When they're ready, set them aside.
4. Sauté the mushrooms: Heat the olive oil over high heat, and toast the garlic cloves in it until lightly golden, about 1 minute. Be sure not to let the garlic burn. Then, add the mushrooms all at once, shaking the pan, and get good color on the mushrooms. When their bulk begins to reduce, drop the butter on top of the mushrooms and let it work its own way down to the bottom of the pan. Add the salt, and cook, stirring often, for 10 minutes. Set aside.
5. Before serving, reheat the mushrooms until they're lukewarm, then toss with the parsley. Spread the toasts with a thin layer of the goat cheese, and top them with a few pretty slices of the shiitake mushrooms.

TIME: *About 30 minutes working time and 20 minutes setup time*
FEEDS: *Should make 50 toasts*
SPECIAL EQUIPMENT: *A 2-inch biscuit cutter, available for purchase at any housewares store. If you wanted to be cute, you could do stars or hearts or something.*

Sweet and Hot Seared Tuna

*T*HIS IS THE big-ticket item for this party. If you're concerned about those who might not like tuna, or want to spend a little less money, this marinade is also delicious on chicken, which can be grilled ahead of time, too. Just don't grill the chicken medium-rare.

10 cloves garlic, crushed

¼ cup fresh ginger, peeled and chopped

1 cup light brown sugar

4 jalapeño peppers, seeded, if you prefer, and sliced thinly

1 cup chopped fresh parsley

Juice of 3 lemons

¼ cup peppercorns, crushed

2 teaspoons kosher salt

½ cup olive oil

6 pounds tuna steaks, cut 2 inches thick

Vegetable oil, for brushing on the grill or grill pan

A handful of parsley, chopped, for serving

Coarse sea salt

1. Divide the garlic, ginger, sugar, jalapeños, parsley, lemon juice, salt, and ½ cup olive oil between two gallon-size resealable bags, then add the tuna steaks, seal the bags, and lay them in your refrigerator. Let them marinate for no more than an hour, or the acid in the lemons will start cooking your fish for you.

2. Heat a cast-iron grill pan, preferably the sort with the ridges, over very high heat for at least 5 minutes before you start cooking. I should warn you that this will be quite smoky, so open your windows if you don't have a proper ventilation hood over your stove. Hold a paper towel, soaked in vegetable oil with a pair of tongs, and brush the ridges of the pan.

3. Take the steaks out of the marinade, and brush off as much of the marinade as you can with your fingers. Lay the steaks in the hot grill pan, regulate the heat a bit, and sear them, 4 minutes per side. This will still give you plenty of rare meat in the middle, but will be a bit more cooked than some people like. If you like the tuna almost raw, reduce the cooking time to 2½ minutes per side. Continue cooking the other steaks, then put the finished steaks in the fridge until you need them.

THE TWO OF US . . . AND FRIENDS

4. To serve, cut them into strips about ½ inch thick, and arrange on a platter. The deep jewel tone of the tuna is like a beacon to buffet guests. Then sprinkle the platter lightly with sea salt, a few flakes of chopped parsley, and a drizzle of olive oil. Serve alongside the Tomato and Snap Pea Salad (see page 258), a green salad, and lots of good bread.

TIME: *About 30 minutes working time, and 1 hour for the marinade. You can make this early on the day you want to serve it.*
FEEDS: *Makes enough for 32 people to have a nice helping*
SPECIAL EQUIPMENT: *A cast-iron grill or grill pan*

MULTIPLICATION TABLE
Tuna for Two

ONE POUND OF tuna steak is plenty for two people, and you need significantly less marinade: 2 garlic cloves, a small slice of fresh ginger, 1 tablespoon brown sugar, ½ seeded jalapeño pepper, a few tablespoons of chopped parsley, a squeeze of lemon, a pinch of salt and pepper, and a drizzle of olive oil.

Tomato and Snap Pea Salad

⊘HIS IS A simple salad, but bright and festive.

16 large beefsteak tomatoes, nice and ripe	1 cup olive oil
5 pounds sugar snap peas, trimmed	Sea salt and pepper
¼ cup Dijon mustard	1 large red onion, sliced into thin half-moons
¼ cup sherry vinegar	A large bunch of basil, leaves washed and dried

1. Bring a large pot of salted water to a boil, and drop in the trimmed snow peas; cook for 2 minutes, until they've turned a shocking green. Immediately drain, and run cold water over them for several minutes to stop the cooking. Dry them by rolling them up in several kitchen towels, and set aside.

2. Core the tomatoes, then cut them into wedges, making sure that the wedges are mostly bite-size (as this is a buffet, making people saw through vegetables with the side of their forks while standing greatly increases the possibility of projectile salad).

3. Make the dressing: Whisk the Dijon mustard with the sherry vinegar, then add a large pinch of salt and several grindings of pepper. Whisking continually, add the olive oil in a steady stream, to help emulsify the dressing. You can make this way ahead, but be prepared to whisk it again at serving time.

4. Platter the salad: Alternate lines of the snap peas and the tomatoes, so that there are rays of bright green and of deep red. Sprinkle crescents of red onion on top of the peas, then tuck whole basil leaves among the tomato wedges. Finally, right before serving, drizzle the whole lot with the light dressing, sprinkling some coarse sea salt on the tomatoes for extra measure.

TIME: *About 30 minutes trimming, washing, and coring time*
FEEDS: *Makes enough for a side dish for 32*

AND BESIDES

*I*T GOES WITHOUT saying that bread would be a good idea. And, if you'd like to serve more, try:

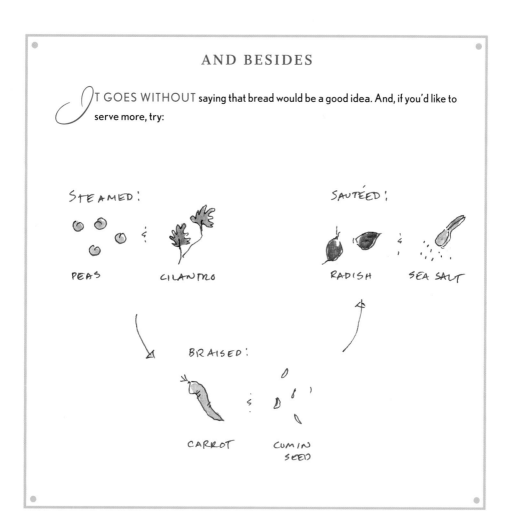

STEAMED:

PEAS & CILANTRO

SAUTÉED:

RADISH & SEA SALT

BRAISED:

CARROT & CUMIN SEED

Blondies with Bittersweet Caramel Crunch

$\mathcal{A}$ FRIEND OF mine—now that I think of it, the same friend who called my beef short ribs "chicken" (see page 67) called these "crack." Again, I think it was a compliment.

3/4 cup whole pecans

3/4 cup whole walnuts

1 1/2 teaspoons baking powder

1 3/4 cups all-purpose flour

Pinch of salt

12 tablespoons (1 1/2 sticks) unsalted butter, softened

1 1/4 cups light brown sugar

2 tablespoons light corn syrup

2 large eggs

2 teaspoons pure vanilla extract

3/4 cup semisweet chocolate chips

1 cup granulated sugar

1. Preheat the oven to 350°F. Prepare a 9 × 13-inch rectangular cake pan by greasing and flouring it. Set aside. While the oven is heating, put the shelled pecans and walnuts on a rimmed cookie sheet or in a pie pan and toast them lightly, about 5 minutes. Pull them from the oven and give them a rough chop.

2. Sift the flour, the baking powder, and the salt together onto a piece of waxed paper, and have it at the ready.

3. In a large mixing bowl or the bowl of your standing mixer, cream the butter with the brown sugar until it is fluffy and evenly light brown. Add the corn syrup and mix to combine. Add the eggs, one at a time, then the vanilla. Add the flour in two additions, making sure to lower the speed of your mixer so you won't have flour everywhere other than in the bowl. When the flour has been evenly combined, pull the bowl out of the mixer, and make sure everything is A-OK by giving the batter a brief turn with a rubber spatula. Sprinkle the nuts and chocolate chips in the bowl, and fold them in. Scoop the batter into the prepared baking dish—it will be quite stiff—and press it into an even layer in the baking dish. Pop it into the oven.

4. Bake the blondies for 30 minutes, checking for doneness using the old clean-toothpick trick. Let them cool in the pan.

5. While the blondies are cooling, begin the caramel: Fill a mixing bowl with ice cubes and set it aside. Pour the granulated sugar into a small saucepan, and drizzle ¼ cup of water over the top. Turn on the heat, and cook the sugar, swirling very gently every once in a while, until it turns a medium golden brown. Remove the caramel from the heat, and immediately place the pan in the bowl of ice, stopping the cooking. After a minute, the sugar will start to become more viscous. At this point, take a dinner fork, stick it in the caramel, and wave it over the blondie pan, allowing little strands of caramel to settle like a spider's web over the top. Do this many times, until there's a pleasing crackle-crust of caramel over the top of the blondie.

6. To serve, cut the blondies into little diamonds.

TIME: *About an hour, partially unattended*
FEEDS: *Makes 32 truly excellent blondies per tray. I suggest you make two batches.*

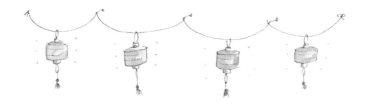

Index